NEWFOUNDLAND

ST. PIERRE
BANK

GREEN
BANK

GRAND BANK

MISAINE
BANK

BANQUEREAU

LAWRENCE JAN ZWART

Adventure

Queen of the Windjammers

Queen of the Windjammers

By JOSEPH E. GARLAND *with* Captain Jim Sharp

Adventure
Queen of the Windjammers

DOWN EAST BOOKS
Camden, Maine

Design by Lurelle Cheverie
Composition by Roxmont Graphics
Manufactured in the United States of America

1 3 5 7 9 8 6 4 2

DOWN EAST BOOKS, CAMDEN, MAINE

To
Lil, Pat and Helen
Best Mates

Contents

Foreword

loucesterman — just the word sends the blood coursing and raises the hair of the neck. The man well versed on the long, able, sleek ones can, with a sharp intake of breath, conjure up all kinds of visions from the past: fleet wooden vessels with enormous mainsails racing through big seas, driving home with the hold fair bursting with fresh codfish. These vessels were the epitome of commercial sail. Some were known for speed, some for their incredible beauty, all were known for their ability. A vessel capable of surviving the fishing grounds of the North Atlantic in winter, of being driven to the limit and beyond to make the market — that's a vessel we bow to. She is able.

My old *Adventure* is one of those. The thought of her still brings me up all standing. She is a survivor, not a vision. She is here, real, and beautiful. She demonstrates each day that incredible mix of beauty, speed, and ability. And I can stand on those decks with a whole-sail breeze, arm hooked into the rigging, and watch her go, watch the miles bubble out from under the stern as they have done now for more than fifty years. She is fantastic!

For the past twenty years, as I pursued the history of this old girl, the more I discovered, the more savory it grew. The inspiring interviews with the old fellows who fished and worked on her generated a passion for this yarn. It became an addiction for which the only cure was this book. The *Adventure* is not only the last of her breed, but even more important, she's one of the most famous vessels in the North American fishing industry. To have set the highline records for all vessels of any type until her retirement in 1953 (over $3.5 million in twenty years alone!) crowns this vessel with an honor to be revered by all who know the sea. She is not just a page out of history, but a monument to fishing tradition. A monument not entombed in concrete, not chained to the dock in a stuffy museum, rotting and trod on by thousands of dirty soles. No, she sails, she lives, she is majestic! Her spirit infects thousands of enthused, experienced and inexperienced sailors who, through her, have become steeped in the kind of voyaging our forefathers did when wind was the only power. We are still living that part of the past — and it is some thrill.

The yarn had to be told in the proper way. It had to encompass all parts, but mostly it had to be told with gusto. It had to convey the stomp of rubber boots on deck and the roar of a fresh gale in the rigging. And the dangers here: black fog, little dories, and men astray; the storms, hull and decks crying with the strain. An unseen rocky ledge splitting up through the heavy bottom planking. The men lost. The sadness. And to do justice to all this, Garland was our man. Sterling Hayden said a mouthful in his introduction to *Down to the Sea* when he wrote, "Joe Garland, I salute you. You've told it like it was!" So, Joe, break out and get on deck. It's your watch!

Captain Jim Sharp

Preface

 othing afloat could have been more hopefully named, or more prophetically, in hindsight, than the subject of this seagoing biography. For nigh sixty years she has been fulfilling both the hope and the prophecy, loosing adventure with all the gusto of her type on all who have sailed in her.

As if this were not enough for any one vessel, in all the time since 1926—the second year of the second Coolidge administration—she has served but four masters, two of them for an aggregate of forty years in two wildly contrasting careers.

All her long and vigorous life—astoundingly long and vigorous for a wooden ship—*Adventure* has been at sea and working every single year but one, and that was an enforced layup at the end of her fishing days due quite simply to the fact that she had finally worn out and outlived her crew.

For twenty-seven years this classic Gloucester schooner reaped the bounty of the North Atlantic banks in the classic way, biblical in its simplicity, until the dying twilight after World War II, when she was the very last, the Old Lady, the living ghost of the once-great fleet of American dory trawlers that put New England on the fishing map of the world.

Yet such was her destiny that after she was retired in 1953 from a fishing career carried on for the most part under diesel power, *Adventure* was reborn as the magnificent sailing vessel she was designed to be and as she started off in life to be. And since then, as the Queen of the Windjammers, she has sailed the Maine coast, smashing along at fourteen knots on the wings of the sou'wester, or ghosting through the fogs, to the ineffable joy of generations of working passengers and the envy of anyone with a grain of salt in his blood who has stood on shore or deck and watched her sweep by with all the grace and power that made *Gloucester* a magical word around the world.

If you have ever seen that great old motion picture of the 1930s, *Captains Courageous*, and if you have an unexplainable yen to know how it was to feel the slanting deck of a Gloucester schooner under your feet, to experience the push and the thrill of the wind and the sails and the heft of the spars that drove these great vessels out to the banks and back in the best and the worst of the weather, to sway up canvas and haul sheets the way the horny-handed gang did in the old days, to spit to leeward and rub up against the life and the hardness and the camaraderie of the dorymen profanely plying their oars and hauling their trawls with many a glance at the lowering clouds—then there is only one route left in all creation, and that is down the gangplank of the schooner *Adventure* out of Camden on the coast of Maine.

Although I've written about the Gloucestermen for many years and tried to recapture some of the essence of their ways, even to skippering my own little schooner yacht for a time, the real feel of the big ones eluded me until I had launched into the research for a book on them in 1981, and Captain Jim Sharp invited me aboard *Adventure* for the last cruise of the summer. Captain Leo Hynes was along for this seasonal finale in his old command, as was by then the tradition, and it was the beginning, for me and my wife, of two extraordinary new family friendships.

Though uncharacteristically windless, that last cruise of 1981 helped fill the sails of the book that emerged three years later, *Down to the Sea: The Fishing Schooners of Gloucester*. And out of that cruise and that book emerged the partnership with *Adventure*'s two skippers that has produced this one.

Most of my work had already been done for me. Jim Sharp had been collecting material on this nautical passion of his for years, culminating in hours of reminiscence and explication by Captain Hynes at the tape machine that without a doubt add up to the most authoritative and extensive (and surely entertaining, for the Old Man is a master raconteur) oral history of dory trawling in the North Atlantic ever recorded.

Not content with cajoling every least detail and last yarn from his mentor, the fourth master of the *Adventure* elicited old-time talk from other survivors of the era—Henry Abbott, John Flannagan, and the venerable Mike O'Hearn—with similarly salty results.

My late good friend Gordon W. Thomas, whose father, Captain Jeffrey Thomas, built *Adventure*, framed the bare structure of her story in his authoritative biography of the Gloucester schooners, *Fast and Able*. As the leading chronicler of the breed, Gordon provided most of the background on the life and career of his famous father and on the early years of *Adventure* in several interviews taped by his son, Jeff Thomas II. Young Jeff added still more to the record with his sessions with the late Captain Angus Tanner of Nova Scotia and Harry Eustis of Gloucester, both old sailing fishermen. As Gordon helped me so often and so generously with the more arcane aspects of many an effort in the past, so Jeff has pitched in with this book on the family boat.

Were it not for the insatiable fascination of the late John Clayton with everything that had to do with the building and the fishing of the Gloucester schooners and the men who worked them, the superbly graphic side of this work would almost be a blank. His documentary trips with oilskins and camera in those closing years as the guest of the prescient Leo Hynes yielded unmatched black-and-white portraits and vignettes of vessel and crew and their ways. Clayton's exciting slides may be the only color photographs ever taken of American dory trawling. In any event, they will remain The Record of the flesh and blood and blue water and white spray of it. His labor of love gives another dimension that nothing else could. We honor his legacy of moments forever lost but frozen in time and are grateful to his widow, Mrs. John M. Clayton II, and to his son, John III, for their permission to reproduce such a unique collection of Americana.

Among other shipmates at various stages during the writing of this book was the Maine writer and editor Peter H. Spectre, who started on the project only to have to drop it because of the pressure of other work, and left behind yet another enlightening interview with Leo Hynes. Tom Fowler, another of Leo's adventurers, gave me a good yarn or two. William P. Coughlin, veteran *Boston Globe* newsman and waterfront reporter and *Adventure* enthusiast, urged the project along and provided valuable research help. Joseph P. Mesquita, Jr., and Mary Mesquita Dahlmer of Gloucester dug up the affidavit of their father, the fabled Captain Joe, on his run-in with the Germans during World War I. To another new friend and *Adventure* shipmate, marine artist Tom Hoyne of Chicago, whose supreme paintings of the schooners at sea set the blood to racing, go our expressions of delight with our book jacket. As so frequently in the past, the resources and cooperation of the Cape Ann Historical Association and the Sawyer Free Library of Gloucester, and the Peabody Museum of Salem, are gratefully acknowledged. And so, too, the friendly and imaginative efforts of Leon Ballou, Karin Womer, Kathleen Brandes, and Down East Books in making this voyage possible and bringing the craft to port.

Such a joy was the telling that I sailed through the whole of it, all fourteen chapters, in a mere twelve weeks and regretted that the end had to come. To celebrate, I sailed again on *Adventure*'s last cruise of the 1984 season with Captain Jim, and again Captain Leo, just turned eighty-four. *This* time it blew, and didn't the Old Lady kick up her heels!

J.E.G.

Eastern Point
Gloucester, Massachusetts
October 1984

The Old Lady

Twenty-seven Greater Boston crew members of the fishing line-trawler Adventure *were in peril aboard the badly leaking craft 40 miles east of Cape Cod late last night, despite the presence of a Coast Guard cutter.*

Earlier reported sinking in heavy seas, the craft was "proceeding very slowly" under escort to Boston as her Melrose captain and crew fought valiantly to save themselves and "The Old Lady"—the only Boston-owned line trawler still in the fishing business.

Boston Globe, April 21, 1948

es, they called her that, the Old Lady, as if she were the mother of them all. Of course the whole coast that was in the know knew what they meant: the big and buxom and still-beautiful knockabout fishing schooner *Adventure* of Boston, originally out of Gloucester, the last of the dory trawlers, the very last. Twenty-two years old was this survivor, this living ghost from the age of commercial sail, old indeed for a hard-worked ship of wood, and every one of her 121 feet showed every day of it. Likewise did her crew. Survivors all, wood and flesh. But with a certain amount of dignity and a hell of a lot of spirit.

Lucky, said some. Jinxed, said others, looking at the down side, workmen who would blame the tool. Where trouble was a way of life, *Adventure* couldn't always *keep* out of it. But once in, she never failed to *get* out of it—with more than a little help sometimes, to be sure. Same for Captain Leo Hynes, who had been in and out of fixes since he first put childish grasp to an oar in the tides of Newfoundland, and his crew of twenty-six hardhanded and softhearted fishermen, walking ghosts from bygone days themselves. Schooner, skipper, and sailors, as the code of the dorymen decreed, *share and share alike.*

This time she had sprung a gusher back in the stern somewhere. The ocean was squirting in like a firehose, sloshing around in the main cabin and the engine room, and the leak, wherever it was, was both inaccessible and unpluggable. Naturally, it was blowing like the devil, seas making up and black o' night, and naturally they were fifty miles out to sea off Cape Cod with 105,000 pounds of fish in the hold, mostly haddock. It was the twentieth of April, 1948. The Old Lady was in a fair way of taking her last bow.

Nine days earlier the old two-sticker with the sheer that made your pulse quicken for all her dinginess had churned away from the Fish Pier, out of Boston Harbor and past that guardian lighthouse with the ominous name, The Graves. Tall masts and a spread of canvas graced her youth, but now, with the war over and the slab-sided beam trawlers and their stinking diesels ruling the fishing banks, wind was more enemy than friend. So *Adventure*'s spars had been topped, and the stubs carried shawls of riding sails as if to steady an old lady crossing a breezy street.

A hundred and eighty miles to the southeast, way out beyond Cape Cod and Nantucket Shoals, lay the western edge of Georges Bank, a vast underwater sandbar swirled up by the mixing of the arctic Labrador Current and the tropical Gulf Stream. Across the deep of the Gully between them, to the northward, lay smaller Browns Bank, halfway to Nova Scotia from the Georges. Prolific feeding grounds, these close neighbors, for cod, haddock, hake, the once plentiful halibut, and other commercially valuable species. And prolific graveyards, with their treacherous shoals and currents, fogs, sudden storms, and overwhelming waves.

Twelve dories and two spares *Adventure* carried in twin nests on deck. Two men to a dory, they dropped over and rowed away as far as the eye could squint, setting miles of trawls with thousands of baited hooks on the bottom. Hauling, slatting them off, rebaiting, filling the dories, pitching them up over the plunging, leaping rail, rowing back out, underrunning again, day and night, fair and foul, twenty-four dorymen.

And back on board, Skipper Leo watching, watching, listening, listening, pacing back and forth, hither and yon, peering, tending his flock. Old Fred Thomas tending his engine as he had since his Old Lady was launched in 1926 by Cousin Jeff. Cook tending his stove for the endless meals, a solid week of it out there.

Coming home it had breezed up from the southwest around noon that day, until by three they had a thirty-knot gale on their hands. That was when Fred yelled up that water was making in his engine room. Leo Hynes ducked below. "My God, it would have scared you to death to see it coming in!" They shut off the main engine and cranked up the small auxiliary that ran the generator and the two bilge pumps. Only one would work. The skipper ran forward and rousted the gang out of the fo'c'sle to turn to at the pair of hand pumps up on deck.

For two hours they pumped but could make no headway. Stuck out there, in danger of foundering, the water threatening the engine, darkness in the offing, the worried captain at five o'clock put out a distress call over his radio. He decided to keep half the gang at the deck pumps and to send the rest below to bail.

Crew member Henry Abbott: "We broke out the floorin' under the after hold—good thing we hadn't put no fish down that hatch—an' got them big coffee cans an' buckets an' filled the haddock baskets an' heisted 'em up an' back down. The baskets warn't very tight, but we kep' 'em a-goin', an' the pumps, an' it didn't gain on us, the whole gang in the hold fillin' an' heistin' an' on deck pumpin' an' a man watchin' fer a bad sea comin' aboard so they could jump fer the riggin'. Gale o' wind. Dark. Jeez, 'twas bad."

Johnny Doran, skipper of the Boston beam trawler *Plymouth*, four hours' steam away, heard *Adventure*'s mayday, got her position, and headed for it full throttle. So did the Coast Guard pocket cutter *General Greene* from Gloucester. Patrol planes from Quonset and Salem took off but never found her.

Adventure had all her deck lights on when, about nine that evening, the *Plymouth* hove up to her windward, providing some lee from the force of the seas and protection for their dories to come up alongside if the Old Lady's men had to give her up. An hour or so before midnight the *General Greene*, ghostly white, loomed up out of the blackness. Johnny and the *Plymouth* were sent gratefully on their way, and the Guardsmen stood by, close as they could hover to windward and maintain steerageway, their Lyle gun at the ready to fire a towline over to *Adventure* if it came to that.

There had been a lull, but now it breezed up again. The fishermen got the two bilge pumps pumping off the auxiliary engine until one clogged and quit. It took them an hour to move a ton of fish out of the way to get it cleared, the gusher gaining all the while.

Bogged down with fifty-two tons of fish and a bilgeful of the Atlantic Ocean careening around inside her, *Adventure* wallowed helplessly. "I was afraid," recalls Leo, "that if it got any rougher we couldn't stay on deck to pump. As it was, I got knocked down once, and my boots were full of water."

To steady their stricken schooner and make some headway, they bent on three riding sails and got her on a course for Boston at two or three knots. Fred Thomas got the engine turning again, slowly. All night they pumped and bailed and hoisted and emptied, the *Greene* hanging to windward. Around eight the next morning the Old Lady eased with a groan of relief alongside the Fish Pier, the weary gang still pumping, and the lumpers jumped aboard to unburden her of her huge weight of fish.

He had just spent ten grand for repairs to the stern, the fagged-out skipper in his watery boots sighed to the newspaper reporters who came down to welcome home these hard-bitten survivors. "I don't know what we'll do with the old thing. Maybe I'll have to give her up."

As it turned out, she hadn't given up on them, and they didn't have to give up on her. They pumped their way the thirty miles or so from Boston back to Gloucester, where *Adventure* was cranked up again on the marine railway. The leak was found and fixed, and in due course they were back fishing.

Nevertheless, burly Leo Hynes, forty-eight years old and veteran of a lifetime at sea, reflected on the inevitable. For fourteen years he had been fishing the old girl and fishing her hard, nursing her along, making her (he and his men, who were about worn out too) the highliner of the fleet. And before him for eight years was Jeff Thomas, bigger and burlier yet, who built her in 1926 and fished her and died at her wheel in 1934. The breed itself had been dying long before *Adventure* slid down the ways, the breed of schooners and men, and she and they were truly half-real, half-ghost, feet in the graves of the past.

The last sailing fisherman, built as much to wrest the coveted racing cup from the Canadian schooner *Bluenose* as to wrest the fish from the sea, was the blueblooded schooner *Gertrude L. Thebaud* of 1930. Hynes had her on a few trips before he took over *Adventure* four years before *Bluenose* beat the *Thebaud* for the final time in 1938, dropping the curtain on nineteen years of hard racing between the fastest schooners of Gloucester and Nova Scotia. The old rivals survived their rivalry and the war, only to leave their bones on the shores of the Caribbean— *Bluenose* wrecking in 1946 at Haiti, the *Thebaud* heaving herself on the coast of Venezuela only a couple of months before *Adventure* came so close to taking the plunge that night in 1948.

A few of the old-time fishing schooners had suffered the shame of having their masts and bowsprits cut off to make beam trawlers of them. More pay for shorter trips, shorter hours, less work, and a hell of a lot less hazard. What could a man do? Who was left to go dory trawling in the time-honored, time-cursed way?

The tedious baiting-up, the back-busting work of rowing the dories laden with two men and their gear and on top of that the fish, the setting of tub after tub of trawl, and hauling back thirty pounds of codfish by ones and twos and dozens, balking every inch up from sixty fathoms and more. Forking them up over the rail of the heaving schooner in a roller-coaster sea, dressing them and icing them and doing it all over again, and managing the vessel. The hardship, the cold, the wet, the slippery, the frozen, the numbing fatigue, the regular screamer of a breeze, the blown-out sails, capsizing or getting run down by your own skipper, or by somebody else, or by God-knows-what in the thick o' fog or snow or night, or going astray forever and starving to death.

Few of the dwindling band of oldsters were thick of hide and hard of head enough to keep on flogging themselves for the sake of the old ways, for the bringing-in with pride of those big, firm, fine-textured fish taken off the hook, unmaimed by

The Gloucester schooner Adventure, nesting fourteen dories on deck and tubs of trawl wherever space avails, churns away from the Boston Fish Pier past a modern dragger around 1949. She leaves Commonwealth Pier to port. The old Customs House Tower still dominates the Boston skyline. JOHN CLAYTON PHOTO

the squeezing mass in the cruel and crushing cod end of the dragger's otter trawl. All for a better price, but what *of* the price?

Damn few of the younger fellows were taking up or going back to dory trawling in the year 1948, especially if they were back from the war and had their bellyful of hardship for a while. So there were only Leo Hynes and his diehards in *Adventure*, Al Hines and his in the little *Marjorie Parker*, built in 1923, and the doyen of the three, the doddering *Gertrude de Costa*, launched in 1912. By 1949 the *de Costa* was retired to Canada, and then there were two. Then Hines and the *Parker* threw in the sponge, and there were only the Old Lady and her dorymen, the ultimate survivors.

■

Toilers of the sea. The first miserable settlement of them in North America scratched a feeble toehold out of the wild western shore of Gloucester Harbor on Cape Ann, at what is now Stage Fort Park, in 1623. English fishermen they were, and in the act of barely surviving their first New England winter they unofficially established the Massachusetts Bay Colony before shifting a few miles southwestward to the more protected shore called Naumkeag by the Indians, Salem by the white men. Before many more years Gloucester was resettled for good, and the fisheries have been pursued there without total interruption ever since.

Salt fish—the gutted, split, and heavily salted slabs of codfish cured in the sun on wooden frames called flakes until hard and tough as an oak plank—was the end product. The pioneers shipped it across the seven seas about as readily as they did lumber, for it lasted like leather and defied consumption until soaked for hours in fresh water. Salt gold it was, the currency of the Bay Colony, worth its weight in anything that could be bartered—from sugar to rum, figs to fine wines, white lace, black slaves, hymns by the trunkful, and spinets to play them on.

The virgin seas off the northeast coast of the New World teemed with the currency, and not just that string of great banks that stretches abreast of the continental shelf from Georges Bank off Cape Cod eastward through Browns, La Have, Roseway, Emerald, Western, Sable, and Banquereau off Nova Scotia to the Grand Bank, grandest of all, off the forbidding coast of Newfoundland. No, a blind man with a bare hook could haul in a doryload of prime haddock way up inside Gloucester Harbor within a stone's throw of the beach, and lobsters were tossed back as pests.

As toehold turned to foothold, and the American colonies commenced to prosper and pay off for the mother country, every harbor worth naming along the coast from Connecticut to Maine sent forth men and boys to fish. Some plied their lines and nets never out of sight of land. Others, like Gloucestermen and Marbleheaders, built strong sea vessels and fared as far as distant, fogbound Grand Bank for weeks and sometimes months at a trip, filling their holds up to the hatches with kenches, or bins, of dressed fish as the salt they sailed with did its work.

Hand-hewn from the backwoods that grudged every board foot they yielded to the settlers, these rough colonial fishing vessels of no more than forty or fifty feet adopted and then adapted the two-masted rig with fore-and-aft sails that was their European inheritance and that proved suited, in a middling way, to the uncertain winds of the northeast coast and the Western Ocean. And so it happened, one fine day in 1713, on the eastern shore of Gloucester's inner harbor, that the ingenious Captain Andrew Robinson launched a fishing vessel in this line of descent that slid so slickly into the tide as to excite one onlooker to exclaim: "Oh, see how she scoons!" Pronounced her maker with semantic ingenuity to match the occasion, "Then a scooner let her be!"

■

The scant surviving records only hint at how the coastal fishing communities suffered from the blockades, the fighting, the naval warfare, and the recruitment drain of the endlessly long Revolution, and suffered all over again during the War of 1812, although in neither conflict were the more daring loath to profit where it profiteth, be it from privateering or smuggling.

As merchant commerce concentrated in Boston and Salem, fishing and the ever-more-complex support system that the burgeoning industry required centered on Gloucester, with its expansive and usually protected outer bay and secure inner harbor, yet easy access to the sea. Marblehead hung in as a stubborn second until a sudden storm took such a toll of her boats and men out on the banks in 1846 that the 'Headers forever abandoned fishing as their main sustenance. Gloucester had the field to herself, and by the latter decades of the nineteenth century she was the busiest fishing port in America and perhaps in the world.

The nets, traps, and weirs of the shore fishermen aside, from the beginning the one-man, one-line, one-hook (or three or four at the most), one-fish, over-the-rail way of deep-sea fishing was the rule.* But then in the 1850s some of the schooners tried carrying dories, those flare-sided, double-ended, flat-bottomed wooden rowing and sailing boats fourteen or sixteen feet long on the bottom that are endowed with the mystical ability to become more stable the heavier they're loaded—within reason. These innovators simply nested a few dories one inside the other on deck and swung them overboard when they reached the grounds. The men would leap in, row off to a likely spot and drop their handlines. Thus were the odds first spread.

At about the same time, however, the more imaginative fishermen were experimenting with the trawl, a tarred cotton groundline heavier than a handline, a mile or so in length, to which were tied at intervals shorter, lighter lines, each with a hook at the end, called gangings. The trawl, with its hundreds of baited hooks, was flicked out of the dory by one man as his mate oared along; then it was anchored and buoyed at each end so they could find it and retrieve it. A pair of dorymen could fish hundreds of hooks at once, a dozen dories twelve times as many.

Old ways die hard among fishermen, but by the 1870s dory trawling was the new way in the banks fisheries (except on the feared Georges, where they stuck to the relative safety of the rail), even as the purse seine that could encompass a school of mackerel (if the netters were quick, clever, and lucky enough) was retiring hand-lining for mackerel at the rail (called jigging) to the lore.

Consigning two men to a chip of a boat on the empty Atlantic a hundred miles from some barren shore was probably no less humanitarian than dropping their landlubbing brethren in Kentucky down a hole in the earth with a pick, a lamp, a ham sandwich, and a canary. Fish and coal were among the sinews of the

---

* The term *highline* is said to have originated aboard these old deck handliners, on which the best fisherman (the high line) was awarded the highest place at the rail, the farthest forward, with no potentially entangling lines upstream of him.

The Old Lady   7

new society, and the cost is not always reckoned as conscientiously as it might be when growth and profit in the name of progress are the order of the day.

So there is some irony to the fact that during this very decade of the 1870s when the owners were pitching their men wholesale into the dories to undertake the most hazardous means of mining the sea yet devised, the schooners they were sending them in were sinking, literally, to the decadent depths of their design.

Broad, shallow, graced with euphonious clipper bows, masts and topmasts reaching for the skies, lunging bowsprits, incredibly long main booms, acres of canvas, wonderfully fast under ideal conditions—and dreadfully dangerous—were the fishing schooners of the 1870s built for fast trips and quick payoffs.

The sad statistic of this frenzied competition is seared in the soul of the city. Between 1869 and 1879 alone, Gloucester lost 195 schooners and 1,285 men. Many of these killer vessels were knocked down by squalls or near-hurricanes or rogue waves and capsized in their roles as dory trawlers, handlining Georgesmen, and seiners. Many of the men who had gone down to the sea went down with their ships, while others were washed or blown or knocked off booms, bowsprits, decks, and rigging, or went adrift in their dories, never to be seen again, or toppled out of them or capsized in them, and were drowned. All this out of a Gloucester fleet of some four hundred schooners.

Here was legal manslaughter and stupidity, in a word, greed, unmatched in the mines or the factories. Revulsion and reform were bound to set in, and they did. By the 1880s vessels of a different shape were sliding down the ways of the saltwater farm town of Essex, where three thousand schooners had been built for neighboring Gloucester since the days of the colony. Vessels with deeper draft, lower center of gravity—more effectively ballasted and conservatively canvased — vessels with a firmer grip on the water. In some respects (since there is nothing new under the sun), here was a rediscovery of the tested sea qualities of the old-fashioned pinkies and Chebacco boats that made up the fleet at the beginning of the century.

The most striking reform, the idea of the Boston fishing schooner designer Thomas F. McManus, was simplicity itself. In 1902 McManus invented the knock-about, or spoonbow, schooner with no bowsprit for a man to get sent out on to handle headsails at the risk of getting blown off or dunked off or washed off by a capricious sea, and no ill-maintained, rotten footropes to give way suddenly under him. In designing the *Helen B. Thomas*, first of the knockabouts and grandmother of *Adventure*, Tom McManus extended the bow almost to the point where the widow-maker, as its potential victims wryly called the bowsprit, would normally end. Allowing for some necessary modifications in balance, the designer preserved with a few deft strokes of his pencil both the sailing qualities of the schooner and untold lives. In the process he expanded the living space in the fo'c'sle.

The late Howard I. Chapelle regarded the knockabout as "the acme in the long evolution of the New England fishing schooner," of which he was the leading historian. The stunning sail carriers with the yachtlike lines and spiking bowsprits that were created in the 1920s quite as much for racing as for fishing were certainly faster, but for safety and reliability, none could match the knockabouts, of which the *Adventure* and the *Gertrude de Costa* were the last of their type.

If Gloucester could look to the shipbuilders of Essex to replace the thousands of schooners lost or worn out over the centuries, she could not look to her own wives and mothers to replenish the legions of men and lads lost or worn out in the fishing of them—3,800 drowned, killed, or missing between 1830 and 1900. But the fishing would go on, and, as to a magnet, the replacements were drawn from both shores of the Atlantic.

First came down the tough and seawise fishermen of Newfoundland and Nova Scotia, where the living was harder even than along the northern New England coast. Then the Irish driven from Galway by the famine, and the Portuguese from the Azores and the mainland, deepwater men all, and the brawny Scandinavians, and finally the Sicilians, the fishermen of the ages. By the turn of the century the majority of the masters of Gloucester's armada of fishing schooners—her cloud of canvas, her cloud of sorrow, her cloud of joy—were what the town called, with a mixture of pride and poignancy, whitewashed Yankees.

For all its excesses and shortcomings, an epoch whose passing would be regretted more than most was on the verge of its finale. Fitting it was that an old lady called *Adventure* would raise the last sail to the sunset.

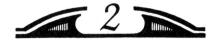

Jeff the Driver

There's only one damn fool carrying all that sail and that's Jeff!

Brother Billy Thomas

eff Thomas was a barrel-chested, iron-jawed, black-mustached, ham-fisted fishing captain in the mold of the whitewashed Yankee who planted close to six feet of bone and muscle in his Red Jack boots. At over two hundred pounds, he would have made a monumental football tackle, in the expert opinion of the Olympic gold medalist and Gloucester writer Jim Connolly, had he attended any but Hard Knocks College. A gentleman was Captain Jeff, they say, and by nature a gentle man. Also a somewhat enigmatic figure. But then, most of the highline skippers out of Gloucester projected that air of being somehow bigger than life. Jeffrey Thomas left hardly more than two personal letters in his own hand and died with those boots on, making *Adventure* the dénouement of his abbreviated life. No less than his peers, he defies typecasting in the dramatic and strangely wistful winding-down of the Gloucester sailing fisheries.

Was Jeff Thomas, when the last sheet was hauled, master of his fate, captain of his soul? If only the venerable craft that has survived the first of her masters by half a century could bear witness. Perhaps she does.

Thomas Thomas was of Welsh stock, and Marthe LeBlanc, French Acadian.

They grew up on diminutive Isle Madame in Arichat, a largely French settlement on the south shore of Cape Breton Island, the dramatic, high-cliffed northeastern bastion of Nova Scotia. They fell in love and married, and she bore him a daughter and nine sons. William Henry (Billy) arrived first, in 1857, and Jeffrey Francis (Jeff), the last, in 1875, which is a considerable span of bearing and rearing a considerable family.

Maritime Canada in those years was suffering through another stretch of harder-than-usual times, and many families sought something greener in the other fellow's yard. When Jeff was three, the Thomases tried Brooklyn, where the green lasted for about three months. Probably because he was a ship's carpenter by trade, Thomas Thomas was persuaded to redirect himself where he should have stopped in the first place, to New England and specifically to Gloucester, where neighbors from Arichat were already establishing themselves in the fisheries, which were always in the market for new bodies—to replace those sacrificed to the seas and the profits therefrom—and new boats in which to send them forth.*

Gloucester was booming a hundred years ago. Six thousand fishermen, in round numbers, out of a city of twenty thousand, roughly, followed the fisheries. You couldn't pin down the figures, because there were so many transients coming and going by sea and land or, between trips, hanging around Fishermen's Corner across from the post office, the bars and the poolrooms and the vaudeville theatres and various other attractions. In 1882 there were forty-six fishing and fitting-out firms, and a constantly growing fleet that couldn't squeeze into the jammed waterfront and so had to crowd the harbor until there was scarcely tacking room in a breeze. Officially enrolled that year: 353 schooners, four sloops, fifty-nine boats of no mean size, and six steamers.

First-born Billy was the first of the Thomas boys to leap into this fray, surfacing as skipper of a Gloucesterman in 1884 at twenty-seven, followed by brother after brother and various cousins as well until they got to the youngest. Jeff, for some unexplained reason, first found a berth driving a bakery wagon and then married Lulu Norwood of East Gloucester in 1892; her father, Clifford, a shore fisherman, got him a job skinning fish at the Reed and Gamage plant.

Not much future there, so in 1898 Cliff Norwood persuaded his son-in-law, who was now at the advanced age of twenty-three, to be the big boy in the class and embark, if a little late, on the ways of the fisherman under Captain Simeon McLeod aboard his old-time shore schooner *Northern Eagle*. When Sim was through with him, the uncommonly powerful and evidently rather taciturn young fellow

*Jeffrey Thomas's obituary in the *Gloucester Times* of March 26, 1934, gives his age as fifty-nine years, one month, and fifteen days when he died on March 24, which would make his date of birth February 9, 1875. It states that he was the seventh son of a seventh son of Captain Thomas Thomas and made several voyages on a coasting schooner with his grandfather. In his monograph on the Arichat Frenchmen in Gloucester (*see* Bibliography), on the other hand, Stephen White gives Jeff's year of birth as 1876 and credits his parents with ten sons. Gordon Thomas and his son, Jeffrey II, remain the main reliance for family material herein.

Captain Jeff Thomas in his shore clothes—complete with "iron derby,"
celluloid collar, and watch chain—poses at the helm of his schooner
Cynthia *in 1910.* GORDON W. THOMAS COLLECTION, CAPE ANN HISTORICAL ASSOCIATION

was graduated to the fo'c'sle of Captain Reuben Cameron's handsome and full-fledged schooner *Grayling*.

Running home for Gloucester on the wild night of November 26, 1898, only about fifteen miles from their destination, they crossed the bow of the snow-white Boston-to-Portland steamer *Portland*, which returned their signal and altered course to clear the *Grayling*. A couple of other schooners espied the *Portland* through the storm, one of the most disastrous in decades, but never saw her again, for she went down with all 176 aboard in what was recorded in the annals as the Portland Breeze. Jeff could not drive that glimpse of her from his mind and ever after wondered why the ghostly steamer hadn't put into Gloucester, so close by, for shelter.

From *Grayling* Jeff moved to the big schooner *Navahoe* under the softspoken but forceful tutelage of Marty Welch, a rising star in the galaxy of master mariners who steered the fortunes of Sylvanus Smith, owner of one of Gloucester's up-and-coming fleets. Captain Welch took a liking to Jeff Thomas, who was eleven years younger and a mite tardy learning the ropes but catching up fast. When he thought his fellow "Bluenose" (jocular jibe at the frosty Nova Scotians) was ready for it, Marty let Jeff take *Navahoe* as transient skipper while he stayed ashore for a trip.

A few trips later, with Marty back at the wheel, Jeff received a crash lesson in what it was all about, fishing out of Gloucester. Statement of Captain Welch for the Gloucester Mutual Fishing Insurance Company, December 26, 1903:

> Left Gloucester December 7, 1903, for a haddock trip with 9 dories and 20 men all told, fitted for four or five weeks. All went well until Sunday December 20 when we were fishing off Beaver Island [about sixty miles up the coast from Halifax] about 12 or 15 miles, with south-easterly gale and rain, weather thick. About 12 o'clock midnight we started to run in, having been jogging on the ground. Bore away for Beaver Island. About ½ past 2 A.M. we had made the outside light and were running for the Bay Light when we struck on Pancake Island ledge, and the sea commenced to break over us. Furled our sails and watched for a chance to get off the vessel. Vessel had fallen over on her side. In about 10 or 15 minutes got clear from her and rowed ashore to Beaver Harbor some four or five miles from where we struck. About ½ past 6 or 7 we rowed back to the vessel in the dories. Found the vessel fast breaking up and had caught afire. We could not board her and returned to Beaver Harbor. Wired owners and Insurance Company and placed salvage in charge of Mr. Humbolt, the harbor master, and left for home Wednesday Dec. 23rd and arrived at Gloucester on late train Thursday 24th. On board at the time of the accident the usual outfits and about 60,000 lbs. fish.*

Something in Jeff Thomas was born to take charge, which had something to do with his mysterious and intuitive ability to smell the wind, pierce the fog, placate the wave, think like a fish, work like a demon, sail like a fool, outguess the price, persuade the gang—and back it all up with his fists if it came to that, which it rarely if ever did because he was a gentle but big man.

So Jeff had not been back in Gloucester long after the loss of the *Navahoe* when Tony Courant, a leading Portuguese captain, asked him to go transient skipper in his *Gossip*. What names they thought of! Later the same year, 1904, he arrived. The venerable Sylvanus Smith, pillar of the fisheries, had for some time had his eye on him and handed Captain Jeff Thomas, at the age of twenty-eight, his first full command, the three-year-old schooner *Arcadia*, one of the earliest of the old man's vessels to carry his fleet trademark, the name ending *-ia*.

Jeff took *Arcadia* mackereling (not very successfully, for he wasn't partial to

---

* It was an unlucky fortnight. Five days before *Navahoe*'s unhappy demise, the *Alice M. Jacobs*, first steam-powered Gloucester fishing vessel, built by Captain Solomon Jacobs, "King of the Mackerel Killers," drove ashore at Newfoundland in a gale and burned in subzero temperature. She was only eighteen months old. Her frostbitten crew barely made it ashore. Eight days after *Navahoe* broke her back, the fishing schooner *Laurel* out of Lamoine, Maine, formerly Gloucester, broke hers on the selfsame ledge trying to make harbor in a blow; her men got ashore too.

seining) and then dory trawling for haddock and shacking—that is, starting a trip salt fishing with a short load of salt, then taking on ice at some Novie port and finishing out with fresh fish and a fast run home to market. *Arcadia*, Captain Jeffrey F. Thomas, was highliner, top catcher of the haddocking fleet in 1905.

Sylvanus Smith built *Cynthia* the next year and turned her over to Jeff. Returning in the fog from her maiden trip mackereling to the southward on April 20, 1906, she struck Romer Shoals in New York Harbor and remained there for two days before a gigantic Merritt-Chapman lighter lifted her off, fish and all, and carried her like a babe in arms into Erie Basin for repairs. Eight months later they did it again, in Boston Harbor, but she floated with the rising tide and sailed into T Wharf leaking five hundred strokes of the pumps an hour.

Chalk it up to experience. For seven more years without serious mishap Jeff Thomas paid his dues with *Cynthia*, chafing at her easygoing turn of speed. Underneath that taciturnity there lurked a free spirit bursting to cut loose. In April 1913 his owners capitulated and gave him their fast schooner, *Sylvania*, and an option on a quarter interest, which he took up. Designed, like *Cynthia*, by Tom McManus, *Sylvania* was built by John Bishop at Gloucester in 1910 and slid into what was then Vincent's Cove but today is the A & P parking lot. Jeff took her over from Captain Lemuel Firth, whose first command in 1901 after he arrived in Gloucester from Nova Scotia was the *J.E. Garland*, named after the author's grandfather.

Sylvania proved just right for Captain Jeff, and he fished her hard—maybe too hard—haddocking winters and shacking summers. On January 26, 1914, trying to make Sheet Harbor, Nova Scotia, in a gale, he drove her up on White Shoal, only three or four miles west of Pancake Island ledge, where *Navahoe* and *Laurel* were wrecked ten years earlier. That section of coast bristles with rocks, and they were doing seven knots and only a few yards off course when they struck. Luck was with Jeff this time. The crew floated *Sylvania* and hailed a tow to Halifax, pumping for their lives, and when they hauled her up on the railway they saw that nearly the entire keel had been torn off.

He drove her, Jeff did.

Jeff and Lulu had two daughters, Florence and Natalie, and a son, Gordon, whom he would not allow to go to sea. Too many Thomases risking their necks already, he decreed. And one gone—Uncle John, drowned in '99 when his dory capsized sailing with Uncle Billy. So the boy lived the life vicariously from ashore, haunted the Gloucester waterfront, absorbed it all, and grew up to be the chronicler of the schooners.

Billy Thomas retired from fishing in 1916. "One of my heroes," Jim Connolly wrote Gordon, "a high line skipper and grand character. He had the most resonant speaking voice! Power and music there." A year or two before Uncle Billy swallowed the anchor, his nephew related, he was hove to in the *Thomas S. Gorton* in a gale off Gloucester—and it took some breeze to make Billy ease his helm. Along came another schooner just cracking off the knots, canvas thundering, spray flying, the gang hugging the windward rail, and they all wondered who it could be. Sizing her up from the distance, Billy turned to one of the boys with a grin and roared: "There's only one damn fool carrying all that sail and that's Jeff!"

And Jeff it was, in *Sylvania*, bound in for market and going like a greyhound.

Only once of record was Jeff upwinded, and that was on his own *Sylvania*. He had taken on young Angus Tanner, down from Lunenburg, Nova Scotia, to try his luck out of Gloucester. It was 1916. Old Angus remembered, sixty-four years later. "We were heading for Boston Light closehauled by the wind, mighty cold. I had the wheel, and Captain Jeff was standing by the companionway. A heavy sailor he was, carried plenty of sail coming in. But when the lee rail became a stranger, and the water hit the lee corner of the cabin house and came back over him and the companionway and me at the wheel, he said to me, 'You better luff her up a little bit!' "

Tanny Tanner was a fast baiter too. One time he was baiting up a tub of

The ill-fated schooner Sylvania, one of Captain Jeff's favorite
commands, dries her sails at the Sylvanus Smith Company wharf in
Gloucester, probably before America's entry into World War I.
Two men on a raft work on her topsides by the main chain plates.
GORDON W. THOMAS COLLECTION, CAPE ANN HISTORICAL ASSOCIATION

trawl on the cabin top, 510 hooks. "Captain Jeff—he was a father to me, never heard him say a cross word to anyone—was in the companionway. I didn't know he was timing me, but he ducked down in the cabin when I was finished to look at the clock and came back up and told me: twelve minutes."

Almost a lifetime later, when his father's last, the *Adventure*, was the last of them all, Gordon Thomas daydreamed in *Fast and Able* of the days of his childhood:

> It seems as if I can see the *Syvania* now, pulling into the Sylvanus Smith wharf, deeply laden with one of her big shack trips. Her sails were neatly furled; her crew lined along the rail, clad in their bright heavy shirts, exchanging greetings with those on shore. When she was made fast and the trip ready to be taken out, I would climb up on the big main gaff, or shinny out on the bowsprit and lie on the furled jib, where I could get a fine view of all that was going on. Everything was thrilling to me, the towering spars with their big black mastheads, the deck and cabin top, piled high with gear, the big coil of cable and the big anchors up forward, the nests of dories; even the loud noise of the big deck hoister was music to my ears.

Across the sea from this placid scene, on the bloody Western Front, 108,000 doughboys on August 19, 1918, were committed to the Ypres offensive that would totter on until the Armistice. That night President Woodrow Wilson cut short a week's vacation a few mansions away from the Gloucester summer home of Colonel E.M. House, his closest adviser, and took the train to Washington.

The next day, the enemy brought the war almost to America's shores in a dying lash of retribution. Prowling the grounds east of Nova Scotia where nearly two hundred and fifty American, Canadian, and French schooners were fishing, the German U-boat 156 captured the Canadian steam trawler *Triumph* and put a German crew aboard.

The first victims of the *Triumph* decoy on the twentieth were the Gloucester schooners *A. Piatt Andrew*, Captain Wallace Bruce, and *Francis J. O'Hara, Jr.*, Captain Joe Mesquita, and three Lunenburg saltbankers. The Huns came up on them, showed their true colors, gave the crews a few minutes to take to their dories, hung bombs under the sterns, and sank all five vessels.

Number six was *Sylvania*. Jeff was ninety miles off Sydney with 35,000 pounds of fresh fish. Along with his usual crew of mostly Arichat Frenchmen were brother Peter, cousin Frank and cousin Fred, who would be his engineer on *Adventure*. All unsuspecting, they were overhauled by the Trojan seahorse, and the first thing they knew, a brace of shots was fired across their bow and a man with a German accent was shouting through a megaphone for the *Kapitan* to row over with his papers.

Oberleutnant Knoeckel gave them ten minutes to collect their wits and their stuff and pile into the dories. The submariners, who Joe Mesquita told somebody afterward had Charlie Chaplin mustaches and needed shaves, attached their time bombs to the stern of Jeff's pride-and-joy and rowed back to the triumphant *Triumph*, while friend and foe, including the U-156 two miles away, watched *Sylvania* explode in a cascade of spray and splinters and take the plunge.

The various castaways from these desperate depredations (there were a few more, but no great dent was made in allied canned-fish production) were plucked up by passing vessels or rowed and sailed to land. All except Jeff Thomas's dory, which had an outboard motor that cousin Fred nursed all the way into the dock at their native town of Arichat, to the incredulity of the local population. As for U-156, she apparently scuttled *Triumph* and headed back for the shattered Fatherland. A few days before the Armistice, the *untersee* raider struck a mine in the North Sea and with her crew of seventy-seven followed the 33,582 tons of shipping she had sent to the bottom.

Back in Gloucester, with the war about over and no vessel to command, Jeff Thomas went over to Gorton-Pew, the industry's major fleet owner and fish processor. (Sylvanus Smith had died in 1916 at eighty-seven, and his company had been bought in early 1918 by Frank C. Pearce.) In the fall of 1918 he took Gorton-Pew's big McManus-designed auxiliary schooner *Benjamin A. Smith*, named for their president, but only until the following January, when the firm launched the *Maréchal Foch* in tribute to the French commander of the allied forces and turned this large knockabout over to him. The *Foch* had a heavy engine that threatened to shake her apart, and late in 1919 Jeff begged off and rejoined the *Smith*.

On December 17, while the *Smith* was fishing in the fog off Liscomb, Nova Scotia, two of the crew went astray in their dory. Jeff cruised back and forth through the thick—to no avail. John Ernst and Howard Penney were the first men he had lost in the seventeen years since he went transient skipper in the *Navahoe*, and it distressed him greatly, though it was no fault of his—just the hazards of the game—to return to Gloucester with his flag at half-mast. He stayed with the *Benjamin A. Smith* until April 1921, when Gorton-Pew gave him their recently acquired auxiliary schooner *Bay State*, another bigger-than-ever knockabout off the McManus board, built in Gloucester in 1912 by Owen Lantz.

While Captain Thomas was having his postwar problems, the racing fever was striking in, as the seiners say, as mysteriously as the mackerel. There had always been impromptu brushes between vessels falling in while bound out or home, and occasionally the fishermen got up a regatta of sorts outside of Boston or Gloucester for a purse, and once or twice even a cup. But there had never been anything international, which meant Canada and specifically Nova Scotia, and most particularly Lunenburg and the "Dutchmen" there, who sent out a major fleet of big saltbankers.

The America's Cup yacht races between Britain and the United States, which had been suspended during the war, were resumed in 1920 with the Yankee defender *Resolute* and Sir Thomas Lipton's challenging *Shamrock* off Newport, Rhode Island.

Puritan *slides down the ways of the James yard and into the Essex River at the moment of her launching on March 15, 1922. Four and a half years later* Adventure *took the same route.* AUTHOR'S COLLECTION

When one brush was called off because it was blowing too hard, the *Halifax Herald and Mail* issued a challenge for a *real* international race between fishing schooners, wind and softies be damned, for $5,000 and a silver cup. The *Gloucester Times* and Gorton-Pew picked up the challenge and sent Marty Welch to Halifax that fall in the fast *Esperanto*. They beat the Canadian trial winner *Delawanna* two straight and carried the cup back to Fishtown in triumph.

The chagrined Novies proceeded to built the giant *Bluenose* right up to the maximum dimensions allowed by *their* rules for the races and launched her at Lunenburg in March 1921. A syndicate of Bostonians had hired the brilliant yacht designer W. Starling Burgess to match them, and *Mayflower* slid in at Essex the following month. In April the defender *Esperanto* was wrecked on dreaded Sable Island, way off the coast of Nova Scotia, the graveyard of the Atlantic, beset by treacherous sandbars, wild currents, and miserable fogs. Boston's *Mayflower* turned out to be so fast even before the trials that she scared the hell out of both Gloucester and Lunenburg, which dominated the race committee, and they hastened to disqualify her as too "yachty" for their rules.

With *Mayflower* out of contention and his *Esperanto* gone, Marty Welch won the Gloucester eliminations in the fall of 1921 in *Elsie* and sailed her to Halifax. There the gallant old working girl, outweighed, outreached, and outcanvased, was overpowered by the bully *Bluenose*, which had of course been built to get the cup back while adhering to the caveat that the eligibles be working fishermen.

The defeat by *Bluenose* of the best that Gloucester could send against her convinced the town that its only hope of recapturing the cup lay in matching the awesome Lunenburger line for line. That winter two syndicates were organized. One got behind Clayton Morrissey, a rawboned and raw-tempered skipper of ability, and commissioned Tom McManus and Arthur Story to design and build the *Henry Ford*.

The rival group of aspirants formed around the hard-driving, sail-carrying Jeff Thomas, who at the time was fishing the *Bay State*. Jeff's backers included brother Billy, the Boston ship chandler Philip P. Manta, and the Atlantic Supply Company, a Gloucester outfitter just put together by Ben Pine, an enterprising Newfoundlander who would rapidly become the most famous American fishing vessel owner and racing skipper of his day as the result of his association with the races.

The Manta Associates, as they called themselves, took one-sixteenth share each, giving Jeff three as master. They engaged Starling Burgess to design, and Everett James at Essex to build, the schooner *Puritan*, named as was *Mayflower* after the America's Cup defenders created by Starling Burgess's father, Edward, one of the great naval architects of *his* day.

And what a beauty! Long and lean, 138 feet from stem to stern, 124 on the waterline, 25½ on the beam, 16 deep, *Puritan* was launched on March 15, 1922, and towed around to Gloucester, where Captain Thomas placed a lucky five-dollar gold piece under each stick before the stepping, all 99½ feet of the mainmast, tallest in port. The *Gloucester Times* reported him as "immensely tickled over the splendid new vessel he is to command." Before sail was even raised, the waterfront was wondering if this might not be the fastest schooner ever built.

The *Henry Ford* was launched into the Essex River on April 11, only to run hard aground on the beach while being towed around the outside of Cape Ann to Gloucester. It took six days to get her off.

The day after the *Ford* was finally hauled around Eastern Point in some chagrin, *Puritan* embarked on her maiden trip halibuting, forgoing the usual owner's trials, perhaps to underline her eligibility for the coming races as a working fisherman. To a stentorian sendoff, she was towed to the outer harbor by the fast converted World War I subchaser 247, owned by the designer's partner, Frank C. Paine. Aboard were Starling Burgess and his friend, the respected designer L. Francis Herreshoff (who is said to have had some hand in her lines), newsmen, and motion picture photographers.

"Well balanced, the *Puritan*, made a pretty marine picture as her new white canvas [8,988 square feet of it] silhouetted against the leaden sky, and she laid down on her rail and showed her copper-colored waterline," reported the *Gloucester Times*. "Her spoon-shaped bow over which there has been comment by fishermen demonstrated its worth, as she plowed through the seas, throwing the spray to either side, and leaving her deck as dry as a chip."

So well balanced was she that Jeff discovered to his delight that she would hold to her course for minutes at a time with her wheel untended. Outside Eastern Point, feeling the full breeze, *Puritan* showed her stuff and walked away from the subchaser, which was crashing along under full throttle at eleven knots. Burgess was tickled; she was a great success, and faster to windward even than *Mayflower*.

Three weeks later, the latest pride of Gloucester was home with 25,000 pounds of halibut. Jeff exulted to the *Times* that she was among the best he'd ever had, fast on every point of sailing, heavy weather and light. Down off Cape Cod they had met *Mayflower* out of Boston and left her in their wake and come off on top of every tiff they had with several of the fleet on the grounds. Nothing tricky about her either. "Every method known to a capable and experienced skipper was tried out to show *Puritan*'s defects and good points. . . . Captain Thomas is a man who knows a good schooner when he sees one and his recommendation of the *Puritan*'s sailing prowess will be received with satisfaction by the designers and builders." So pronounced the newspaper.

On the twelfth of May she was off on her second trip, shacking. She took out 40,000 pounds of fresh halibut and 11,000 of salt fish in Boston on June 10. Back in Gloucester, Captain Jeff told the *Times* man on the fifteenth that "he felt satisfied he had a vessel that would show them a thing or two, and was itching for the gun that would send him off in the elimination race here this fall. 'In heavy weather the *Puritan* will do her best,' said the skipper, 'but any kind of a breeze is good enough for me. Those spars of hers are so high that the slightest breeze will fill our topsails and drive us along at a good clip, although we haven't really had a good opportunity to see what she can really do as yet. There ought to be some fun here this fall,' said Capt. Jeff as he gazed aloft, 'for there are some crack sailers going out of here now and the race ought to be interesting. The *Puritan* is a roomy vessel, a good sailer, and a good vessel for fishing.' "

Jeff wasted no time between trips. Never been seasick in his life, he'd say, but he could sure get landsick. Late in the afternoon of June 17, 1922, they were off for Boothbay Harbor, Maine, to take on bait and ice. Billy Thomas was along for the ride on this first leg. Among the crew were brother Peter, the cook, and three cousins, including Fred. The wind was fair, and the skipper telephoned home when they reached Boothbay, a little over five hours later. *Puritan* had averaged 14¼ knots, which was thought to be a record for the run and certainly mighty fast for a fishing schooner.

"At the height of the breeze," Jim Connolly wrote Gordon Thomas years later, quoting Ken Ferguson, a Gloucester banker, who was along for the run, "your father

**Beautiful Puritan, *perhaps the fastest schooner of them all,*
smashes along on her maiden trip off Gloucester on April 17, 1922.
Jeff Thomas *has the helm. Every stitch of canvas but her fisherman's*
*staysail—all new and yet unstretched—is set and drawing.***
L. FRANCIS HERRESHOFF PHOTO, DANA STORY COLLECTION

climbed atop of the lee dories and called out: 'Let her take out and find out what she's good for.' She took it. She was what you claim for her, the best all-round sailer in the world up to that time—of two-stickers, yacht or merchant vessels."

Jeff put his passengers ashore at Boothbay Harbor, baited and iced, and at eleven in the morning on June 21 headed for the Grand Bank, sailing by dead reckoning along a charted compass course by logged speed and elapsed time, heaving the lead to check depth when on soundings.

They had crossed the Bay of Fundy and were well along off the coast of Nova Scotia on June 23, their third day out. It had come in thick o' fog on the heels of a strong following southerly, building heavy swells. *Puritan* was rollicking at close to ten knots, easy as could be. At about seven in the evening, with most of the men below, Peter Thomas remarked that they'd probably be off Sable Island by morning.

Half an hour passed. Captain Jeff, at the wheel, reckoned it might be a good idea to take a sounding. He turned the helm over to Anthony Burke, started down the companionway, and his feet no sooner hit the cabin floor when he was knocked off them. She struck like a railroad train and bid up hard, lurched, and hove over on her port bilge. Up forward in the fo'c'sle they were thrown all around, couldn't believe it, had heard no fog signals, thought she'd been hit by a steamer. With the water pouring in, they rushed up the gangway.

There could be no doubt where they were. The fastest schooner ever built had just wrecked herself proving the claim. God only knew how many miles ahead of her course, she had thrown herself in all innocence on the northwest bar of Sable Island with such force that she had broken her back and fetched up on the other side of it, where she now lay, expiring in the sand, the waves breaking over her.

Incredibly, a tremendous length of keel had been torn loose and floated to the surface alongside. *Puritan's* rudderpost was driven clear up through the wheelbox by the impact. Down below, the cabin floor was already awash. The seas crashed across the deck. Night was almost upon them.

The crew was hardly able to get a dory over. One capsized as the three men who had jumped in tried to pull away from the wreck. Two were hauled back in over the rail. The third, Christopher Johnson, drowned before they could grab him.

Jeff Thomas and Israel Larkin leaped in another dory. A sea lifted it up on the rail and washed the skipper overboard. The next one washed him back. Brother Peter collared him, and they got clear.

Jeff and seven of his crew in three dories landed the next morning on the western tip of the desolate island, where they were taken in by the superintendent in charge of the lifesaving station and light. After several days the surf abated, and the U.S. Coast Guard cutter *Tampa*, responding to a radio call, was able to approach shore and take them aboard for home.

The other fifteen crewmen rowed and sailed four dories all night and most of the next day through the seas and the fog fifty miles in the direction of Whitehead,

Nova Scotia. They had a compass and a flashlight but neither food nor water. Then it scaled up, and they were spotted by the inbound fishing schooner *Coral Spray*, which took them into La Have.

"Surely," Jim Connolly wrote the skipper's son thirty years later—and he was not alone in the hindsight—"the Cup would be back in Gloucester for good if she had lived."

And so would Chris Johnson.

Jeff Thomas, back in Gloucester in a few days with the rest of his crew and no *Puritan*, gave out no more newspaper interviews.

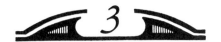

A New
Adventure

I hope I hit that thing!

Natalie Thomas at the christening

ll who had anything to do with her, all whose hearts leaped when they watched her spanking along in the sou'wester, all who had pinned their hopes on her—her owners, her designer, her builder, her crew, indeed all of Gloucester—were stunned by the thunderbolt of *Puritan*'s death three months after her launching. But whose could compare with the emotions of her master, who, that fatal night, as the laws of man and sea decree, had the whole responsibility for her?

Ah, but Sable Island. The Graveyard. Gloucester knew. Thirteen months previously, the first winner of the cup, *Esperanto*, struck a submerged wreck near Sable's southwest bar in the fog and sank in twenty minutes. Four months after *Puritan*, the *Maréchal Foch*, Jeff Thomas's former command, would come to grief on Sable. Five years hence, *Puritan*'s direct successor, the consummate *Columbia*, on which more vain hopes were hung, would hurl herself on Sable in a terrible gale and eliminate twenty-two men without a trace.

Sable was a black word in Gloucester. For the skippers who survived, there

**Oilskinned and booted, Captain Jeff Thomas talks it over with his bos'n,
Emory Doane, by the main cabin trunk of the schooner** Oretha F. Spinney,
about 1924. ATLANTIC FISHERMAN, VOL. 6. JEFF THOMAS II COLLECTION

were nightmares but no apologies, no alibis. Gloucester understood. And no interviews. Instead, the *Gloucester Times* offered an editorial of condolence:

> The disaster to the *Puritan* brings up again to mind that strange bank of sand and fog in the Atlantic, Sable Island. Perhaps with the exception of the Goodwin Sands in the English Channel, it is the deadliest spot to navigate in the world. For centuries, or ever since the discovery of the Grand Banks, it has stood in the way of fishermen. If the alert captain of the *Puritan* was not able to avoid it, what chance did the Portuguese and French captains have three centuries ago when they brought their ships to the Grand Banks to supply fish for the Catholic countries?... The island is a bugaboo to all mariners within five hundred miles ... surrounded by wrecks of every description. The waters are black with them. Treacherous shoals exist for miles about the island and they are constantly shifting. ... Sable Island is the most deadly fascinating and mysterious place on our coast. And now it has swallowed our best aspirant for cup defender.

The wishful editorialist of course meant cup *challenger* and left unasked the nagging question: Jeff, how could you have let her, the fastest we may have ever had, take you *hours* ahead of your course in the fog when you knew what dangers lay ahead?

"A real flying fool, tricky and hard to handle," wrote Gordon Thomas many years later. "You just could not hold her down. . . . This vessel was so tricky she had overrun her course by 20 miles." His father didn't like her, he claimed. She was built to race, was too fast for a fisherman, would run down her dories trying to pick them up.

If so, Jeff's opinion expressed to his son belied his effusions in the press.

Where *did* they think they were just before *Puritan* hit? As reported by a crew member to the *Times*, brother Peter ventured the guess that they'd be off Sable by morning—ten hours and ninety or a hundred miles ahead, in that case. Cousin Fred conceded thirty years later that she was sailing much faster than they realized and that they missed on their dead reckoning. But were they trailing their taffrail log, which is an accurate gauge-at-a-glance of ground covered, plus or minus the tidal current?

The plain fact is that Captain Jeff, like many another able skipper who has run afoul of Sable Island and its currents and bars in fog and dark and storm, didn't know *where* the hell he was that night.*

Back in Gloucester, said his son, Jeff had a falling-out with some of his partners in the late *Puritan*. He came home one night and said, "I'm all through with racing. Don't want no part of it." Gordon suspected that Ben Pine had something to do with it. What his son evidently didn't know was that nine days after Jeff returned to Gloucester from the disaster for which he was responsible, the *Times* reported that Ben Pine had asked him to take over the *Elizabeth Howard*, another very big McManus schooner built in 1916. She was being refitted by Atlantic Supply for Jeff's specialty, halibuting, and painted white. Captain Thomas, the paper said, might sail her in the cup trials in the fall.

Whatever happened, Jeff couldn't have remained in the *Howard* for long. Before 1922 was out, he had gone back to Gorton-Pew, which gave him the *Corinthian*. Piney was at the helm of the *Elizabeth Howard*—the "Gray Ghost" they tagged her, so fast was she in light airs—during the October cup eliminations that were won by the *Henry Ford*. Thirteen months later she was a ghost for real, wrecked on Porter's Island, Nova Scotia, in November 1923.

Long after his great fisherman of a father was a ghost himself, the son—who was raised by his mother to love birdsongs and sunsets and the gentle life at the edge of the tide—persisted in defending the man and blaming the vessel. He needn't have. Each stands on the record.

Ever the moneymaker, Jeff Thomas worked Gorton-Pew's *Corinthian* for a few trips, then their *Elmer E. Gray*, a tough old-timer, narrow as a wedge, built back in 1903 for brother Billy, who used to say that he'd crossed Georges Bank on a plank, she was so sharp. Toward the end of 1923, at the behest of Captain Lemuel Spinney,

* One night in *Adventure*, doing nine knots under power, Leo Hynes laid a course well clear of Sable. Next morning he sounded, found the water alarmingly shoal, and altered course. They had been overhauled so rapidly by the tidal current, he figured, that he was twenty-five miles off his presumed position. They must have just missed the bar, and if the wind had risen during the night, they could have piled up on the island.

a highline halibut catcher and a fellow Novie who wanted to stay ashore for a spell, Jeff took out his *Oretha F. Spinney*, a large knockabout schooner on McManus lines (who else's?) built at the James yard in Essex in 1920. He liked the *Spinney*, an able and conservative seaboat—for he was pushing fifty himself now—and he fished her until 1925.

That year, on January 27, returning from haddocking and bowling along in a choppy sea fifty miles east of Cape Ann, the *Spinney* gave one of those unexpected lurches and a man pitched overboard. Eli Goodick was his name, twenty-seven, with a wife and kid, from Salem. Jeff searched and searched, but the poor soul had drowned without a trace. Flag half-mast again.

Captain Lem returned to the *Spinney*, and Captain Jeff took over the smaller schooner *Falmouth*, built by the James yard the previous year for United Fisheries. No matter what, in Gloucester there would always be a vessel for Jeff Thomas.

But there was something about the *Oretha F. Spinney*. She suited him to a T. He had some money saved (Fred Thomas said his cousin mortgaged everything he owned), and he got the backing of his friend Phil Manta, the Boston chandler, and others, and that early spring of 1926 Jeff went over to the James yard on the Essex causeway to see if they couldn't build him a big knockabout on the lines of the *Spinney*.

They could, and the keel of the first vessel that Jeff Thomas could really call his own, his fifteenth command in twenty-six years, was laid in April.

Landbound and sea-dreaming at nineteen, son Gordon had sketched for his own amusement a fleet of schooners with imaginary names. One evening Jeff asked to look them over for inspiration, for he was superstitious about family namesakes. One called *Adventure* caught his fancy. "Fishing is an adventure," said he, "and I don't believe there was ever a vessel out of Gloucester with that name."*

There were two yards left in Essex, those of the Burnhams and the Adamses having faded from the scene. Arthur D. Story's, the most productive of them all, was (and is today) at the north end of the causeway at the bend in the Essex River, hard by the town center. That of John F. James and Son, in the family under various names since 1850, was southeast off the causeway a couple of hundred yards from Story's.

Between James and Story, ten fishing schooners were built in 1924—and not one wooden beam trawler. The next year produced eight sailing fishermen and the first three of the chunky trawlers designed strictly for power, known in Gloucester

* There hadn't been such a vessel for a hundred and thirty years anyway. The last previous schooner *Adventure* was built in Newbury, up beyond Essex, in 1796. The first schooner of that name was launched in 1787 at Kingston, on Plymouth Bay, for Daniel Rogers, Gloucester merchant and shipowner and the author's great, great, great, great-grandfather. She was half the size of the 1926 version, 53½ tons, 57½ feet long, sixteen feet two inches beam, and six feet seven inches deep. This first *Adventure* of them all was around at least until 1804, when she is last recorded as clearing American customs.

by the descriptive epithet *dragger*. In 1926 *Adventure* was one of five schooners and two draggers. The year after there were eight and seven, then five and eight, and in 1929, eight schooners and six draggers. In 1930, the first year after the Crash, under the fading momentum of a false prosperity, four draggers and six schooners were built, including the *Gertrude L. Thebaud*, last full-rigged fishing schooner.

Power had triumphed by insinuating itself into the bowels of the sailing ships. *Columbia*, back in 1923, was the last schooner launched without an auxiliary engine, an "iron jib"—or, in the case of the schooners increasingly rigged without topmasts for greater stability, ease of handling, and safety aloft, the "iron topsail" when the wind gave out.

The old skills were still there, however, handed down through the generations of Essexmen who built the schooners, paralleling the seamanship and fish sense passed on from old hand to greenhorn by the Gloucestermen who sailed them. Jeff Thomas's new vessel was put together of the same materials, by the same methods, and with virtually the same tools (the first steam-powered bandsaw wasn't let into town, and even then with many misgivings, until 1884) as the thousands of her predecessors that passed with the tide down the Essex River for their outfitting over the previous 250 years or so.

Like the thorax built on the backbone, *Adventure*'s ribs, her frames, rose up on her keel, which was a composite of a couple of mammoth lengths of oak scarfed together by the union of complementary horizontal bevels and laid at a slight incline toward the mother waters on the crosspieces of the building ways.

These frames were the essence of her. They made her shape, and theirs was created by the wisdom and the poetry of her designer. Therein lurked the secrets of her capaciousness, her stability, her ability against wave, collision, ledge, and sandbar, her speed, and—who knows?—her longevity.

For she had the right genes, *Adventure* did. Her prototype, the *Oretha F. Spinney*, was the creation of Tom McManus of Boston, built by the same yard six years previously and no doubt moulded by Essex's virtuoso of that art, Archer B. Poland. The mould was a construction pattern of light wood fashioned to the exact dimensions of each frame over the lines that the moulder had enlarged from the designer's plans to life size on the floor of his loft. From each mould the carpenters sawed and fitted together in precise replication the interlocking pieces of each frame. The *Spinney*'s moulds must have been saved by Poland or by the builder and dusted off for *Adventure*.

Jeff decided, in fact, to deviate only very slightly from the *Spinney*'s lines. Two or three frames were left out to shorten the clone's overall length a trifle, to 121.5 feet, although the waterline lengths of the two remained nearly the same: *Adventure* was 107 feet, the *Spinney*, 107.2. Captain Thomas broadened his version in the quarters a little, giving her 24.5 feet of beam, six inches more than the *Spinney*'s, and reduced *Adventure*'s depth by two, to 11.1 feet. Howard I. Chapelle,

A COOPER-BESSEMER DIESEL PLAYS A PART IN "CAPTAINS COURAGEOUS"!

The Oretha F. Spinney was the sure-enough fishing boat of Capt. Carl Olsen, out of Gloucester. Fit in every way, carrying her canvas prettily, and with a stout Cooper-Bessemer Diesel below deck — to make her independent of weather — she took the eye of Metro-Goldwyn-Mayer. That engine . . . *right* for her old trade . . . *proved anew* in her long run to Catalina . . . will *still* serve her well when the need arises!

Convenience, Economy and Reliability are qualities of Cooper-Bessemer Diesels that mean Fishing Boat Earning Power. Write us for full information.

The brave schooner "We're Here" of the new movie "Captains Courageous" — formerly the Oretha F. Spinney of Gloucester. Powered with a six-cylinder Cooper-Bessemer Diesel Engine, Type FP-6-DR, 180 H.P. at 350 R.P.M.

THE COOPER-BESSEMER CORPORATION

Mt. Vernon, Ohio — PLANTS — Grove City, Pennsylvania

| 25 West 43rd Street
New York City | Mills Building
Washington, D. C. | Hoffar's Limited
Vancouver, B. C. | 53 Duncan Street
Gloucester, Mass. | Esperson Building
Houston, Texas | 640 East 61st Street
Los Angeles, Calif. | The Pacific Marine Supply Co.
Seattle, Washington |

the supreme technical historian of the fishing schooners, had something to say about the implications of this not-uncommon practice:

> McManus often complained that his designs were 'stolen'; that is to say, a design was purchased from him and a vessel built, then if the vessel were successful or outstanding, other vessels were built 'on the moulds' without any design royalties being paid to him. Alterations in design would naturally take place in this stage and this was probably done in the mould loft if the alterations were more than adding a frame space or two. . . . Moulds made from his designs were often retained in the loft, or in the shipyards, and some of these moulds were turned over to McManus, but moulds were too large and awkward to store, so full sets of moulds were often available for unauthorized use.

It is doubtful that Tom McManus received any design royalties for *Adventure*, since she has never been officially documented to him, and Jeff's minor changes were ad-libbed, to put the matter delicately. He first intended her as a ten-dory halibuter. So Fred Thomas claimed. Presumably he decided during construction to add two dories so he could go haddocking too, with four more crew. Lem Spinney was a halibut catcher, content with appropriately smaller accommodations on his vessels. According to Fred, Jeff lengthened the forepeak in order to install two additional bunks, for a total of eighteen in the fo'c'sle, and squeezed in two more to make nine in the after cabin—all by adding one or two more frames.

However, Fred Thomas's version of this likely plagiarism, reported by John Clayton in 1952, does not entirely square with the comparative measurements of the two vessels. *Adventure* was a shade shorter and grossed 130 tons, compared with the *Spinney*'s 134.4. Yet the *Spinney*'s cargo measurement was much greater—eighty-seven net tons against *Adventure*'s sixty-two—suggesting that Jeff paid Paul of the forepeak by robbing Peter of the fishhold; if anything, he *dropped* a couple of frames from the *Spinney*'s plan. He was probably trying to get more for his money, since builders charged by the running foot.*

Such fiddling with the designer's intentions naturally wrought subtle changes in a vessel's performance as well as her layout that were rarely predictable, though not invariably for the worse. Each of *Adventure*'s frames is a subtly different cross section of her hull at that point. The sectional curves vary widely—from the tight,

---

* The rule haunted McManus after he designed the first knockabout, the *Helen B. Thomas* (no relation); her stem extended to the end of her imaginary bowsprit in an exaggerated overhang that gave her the look of a creature about to take flight from the water. The costs of all this extra length were frowned upon, even by owners convinced of the merits of the knockabout, and McManus's subsequent designs reduced the overhang outside and increased the overhead inside the fo'c'sle, where it counted.

Opposite: **Adventure***'s older sister, the* **McManus-designed knockabout** **Oretha F. Spinney,** *is featured in her role as the* **We're Here** *in the motion picture* **Captains Courageous.** *The advertisement is from the June 1937* **Atlantic Fisherman.** *SHARP COLLECTION*

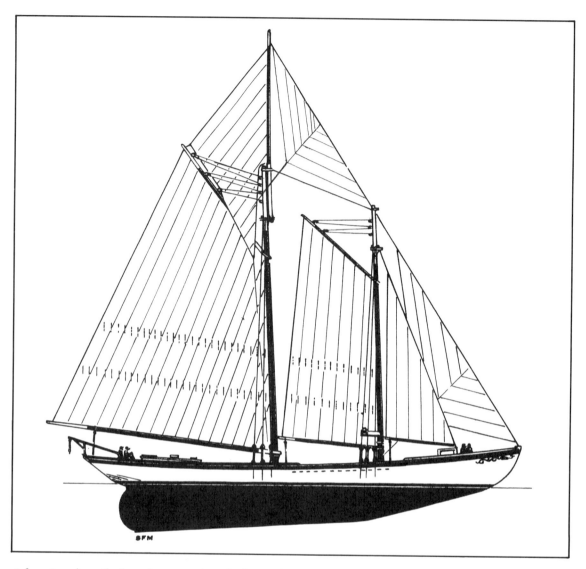

**Adventure's sail plan shows mainsail, foresail, jumbo, and jib—
and aloft, the main topsail and main topmast staysail, her "kite."**

shallow tumblehome at the very stern, through the broad, full, deep contours amidships, where she carries her cargo, and the ever-steeper, narrower, flatter shape of the forefoot to the long, slicing, streamlined knockabout bow.

In order to manage such complex curves in wood, the frames are made up of as many as eleven pieces at the midsection, starting with the heavy crosswise floor that rests on the keel and working up either side, each overlapping the other, through the navel timber, the first and second futtocks, or flitches, the top timber, the planksheer, and ultimately the stanchion above the deck. These were laminated into an immensely strong and rigid unit by boring through-holes and fastening them with pounded trunnels (as long usage corrupted the pegs of locust called treenails). As each successive frame was finished on the ground, the cry went out, "Frame-up!" and the rest of the workers would drop what they were doing and muster to carry it to its place on the keel, raise it, and secure it temporarily with battens.

Most of *Adventure*'s frames are extra heavy—six inches as cut but twelve wide when doubled up, varying in thickness from five inches at the deck to a foot or more at the keel, and spaced but a foot apart. After they were in place, they were bolted through the keel. Then the great oak stem piece, all scarfed, was hoisted up on a pair of shears and bolted to the keel, pointing superciliously at the Essex causeway and the passing, pausing Model-T Fords. And then the sternpost was raised upright and the deadwood timbers filled in and fastened ahead of it to the keel, the graceful transom soaring above the high water of the creek.*

The frames at the extreme ends, the cants, were beveled and bolted to the stem and stern pieces, after which the heavy laminated keelson was laid over the floor timbers and bolted clear through the keel, tying everything together and doubling the backbone.

A few courses of battens called ribbands were next nailed lengthwise to the frames (which were temporarily secured athwartships as well) to hold them in place, and the "dubbers" went to work with adze and shoulder power, dubbing, fairing off the outer surface so that every plank would lay against every frame as it should. Then came the planking, a complex procedure involving carefully worked out "lining" for taper with the changing shape, and reliance on the steam box and a battery of great clamps to twist the hot, damp, limbered board around the hard bends while it was trunneled. White oak three inches thick, as wide as eighteen, and up to forty feet long, shaped with not a half-inch to spare. A job requiring the eye of a Hepplewhite and the arm of a Hercules!**

As each plank, or strake, was laid, fitted, and clamped, the borer moved along with his hand-cranked auger, a penny a hole, four holes to a frame, each trunnel pounded home through the frame by the "driver," sawed off flush, and the head split and wedged to hold forever, if need be. And then on to the inside planking, the ceiling: hard pine, and in *Adventure* all of four inches thick and up to ten wide, more loosely fit to let air circulate, and trunneled. Doubly strong now, she has taken her full shape.

---

* At least some of the framing, Jim Sharp was informed by a member of the James family, was of a special "blue-white oak" cut in Taunton, south of Boston, and was left over from the smaller schooner *Roseway*, launched by James only the previous November 21. Leo Hynes heard that her timbers were so extra-heavy because a number of them were originally intended for a large three-masted coasting schooner. Perhaps the result is a mixture. A lot of the oak, Sharp was told, came out of West Virginia, where they were clearing for the Skyline Drive through the Blue Ridge Mountains.

**Howard Chapelle inspected *Adventure* and made numerous measurements while she was at the Boston Fish Pier on August 5, 1934, and again when she was hauled out. He included several of them in his definitive *The American Fishing Schooners 1825-1935*. Chapelle counted twenty-one strakes from her keel to her deck, varying in width from eight to eighteen inches, all of which he described as of yellow pine (page 567), perhaps erroneously; Sharp found her all white oak–planked when he bought her.

Next came the massive oak deckbeams supported by the heavy "clamp" plank secured the length of either side to the top of the frames above the ceiling. The deckbeams are faintly arched, or cambered, to shrug off water through the scuppers. At about amidships James's men slid in the aptly named great beam, or break beam, the mightiest athwartships support of the deck and topsides, close to the mainmast, the point of severest strain. It serves as well to mark the break, the step from which the quarterdeck rises aft to the stern; this elevation raises the view from the helm and increases the sheer and hence the freeboard aft to the taffrail and the headroom in the main cabin. As the deckbeams were cut and hove aboard, room was left for the main cabin trunk, hatch, companionway, and mast openings, which were framed in with the longitudinal timbers called carlings.

On to the decking of white pine three inches thick, four or five wide, laid on either side of the strongback, or mast bed, which imparts to the entire topside structure great additional strength against the enormous strain of the spars while under sail or in a seaway. *Adventure*'s strongback (measured by Chapelle) consists of a twelve-inch plank along the centerline and two eight-inchers on either side— forty-four inches wide altogether and four inches thick. Around the edge of the deck, at the base of the bulwarks, run the waterways, heavy planks following the curve of the topsides.

Coamings, hatches and hatch covers, cabin trunk, companionways, hawse-pipes, rails, pinrails, sheet horses, deck blocks, stovepipes, rudder, wheelbox, windlass, chainplates, penboards, and deck pumps. Iron Stoddart steering wheel shafted and secured, trademark of the Gloucesterman.

The outboard joiners planed the hull lengthwise and crosswise, traversing, every stroke by hand. The clarion clank of the mallet, the beetle, rang through the yard as the caulkers attacked the seams with two or three miles of oakum, then caulked the deck and payed it with pitch. Down below, the inside joiners set up the bulkheads between fishhold and living space: main cabin with lockers and bunks for Captain Jeff, Bos'n Emory Doane, Engineer Fred, and a chosen few, with nice touches of cypress and fiddleback maple. Ahead of that, the engine room. The long, nervous, pinpoint boring through the deadwood for the shaft. Fuel tanks. Stern bearing. Propeller.

A second bulkhead separates off the cavernous fishhold, capacity 160,000 pounds in the pens, ceiling here of hard pine caulked and sheathed with tin for more effective cleaning. Then the forward bulkhead and beyond that the gangway, the galley, the big black woodstove, the wood locker, food and stores lockers, ice chest, counters. The fo'c'sle, with a long, tapered table ahead of the foremast, bunks stacked on both sides of the bow and right up into the peak, into the eyes of her.

About the time the keel was laid in April, Captain Jeff had returned to halibuting in the *Elmer E. Gray* for Gorton-Pew. But as *Adventure* materialized on the stocks that summer of 1926 he was keeping an eye on every detail, beating a

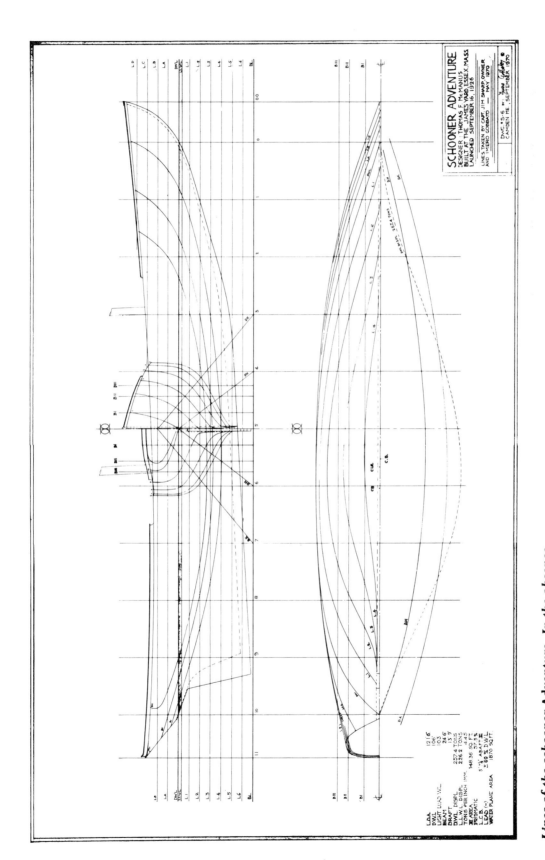

Lines of the schooner Adventure. In the absence of any original drawings, Captain Jim Sharp and naval architect Imero Gobbato measured her in 1970.

path back and forth between the Thomas frame house in Washington Square, three blocks from the waterfront, and the James yard.

By the end of August, she was nearly finished—deck oiled, deck structures and bulwarks white, waterline struck, topsides black, varnish and stain and white paint below. Moving into September, her bottom was painted with red copper antifouling compound that without a doubt came from Tarr and Wonson's red factory, a landmark on the end of Rocky Neck in Gloucester Harbor.

Ready to go. Straining at the gate.

Announcement of impending event, *Gloucester Times*, September 15, 1926:

WILL LAUNCH NEW SCHOONER

Schooner *Adventure*, being built at Essex for Capt. Jeffrey Thomas, will be launched from the yard of James & Son at high tide tomorrow evening.

High water the evening of September 16 was at 7:19, twenty-seven minutes after sundown. That's calling it pretty close for a daylight launching.

The James gang sawed through the ways. She creaked, started, and began to slide. Gordon, who named her, and sister Natalie, who would make it official, were stationed way up in the bow. Natalie was twelve. She gripped the bottle. "I hope I hit that thing!" she prayed. Later she recalled, "The idea that it was champagne didn't impress me. I was just so worried I wouldn't crack it!"

She swung, and cracked it, and in a spray of bubbly she shouted, "I christen thee *Adventure*!" Down slid Captain Jeff's prides and joys, all three of them together, and hit the river with a splendid splash and a rousing roar from the crowd.

Birth announcement, September 18, 1926, *Gloucester Times*:

Sch. *Adventure* was launched from James's shipyard Thursday. A thousand or more spectators witnessed the event.

Fisherman's Luck

The new sch. Adventure, *launched at Essex last week for Capt. Jeff Thomas, is still in the river at Essex awaiting a favorable turn of wind and tide to be towed to this port for her outfitting. The bar at the mouth of Essex River is so roughened with surf that to tow the craft down would be difficult. The* Adventure, *built along the lines of sch.* Oretha F. Spinney, *only a few feet shorter, will be ballasted at Chisholm's wharf and will be fitted for winter haddocking by Capt. Thomas.*

Gloucester Times, September 21, 1926

is newborn vessel was stuck up in the river like Moses for six days while Jeff chafed, but with the memory of the *Henry Ford* so ignominiously aground on Coffin's Beach on her tow-around in 1922, they waited. Not until March 23 could the *Gloucester Times* report that *Adventure* had been towed down the six-mile sliver of tidal river through the salt marshes, out into broad Ipswich Bay, clear around Cape Ann, and up in by Eastern Point to Gloucester Harbor. Chisholm's now being unavailable, she was laid alongside the Independent Fisheries wharf for the ballasting, riding as high as a cork.

Thirty-five tons of pig iron were stowed into the bilges, deep as they could be packed. To keep this stabilizer from tumbling around in a most destabilizing

Just towed around from her launching at the James yard in Essex, Adventure rides high in Gloucester, evidently unballasted as yet, probably at the Independent Fisheries wharf, in September 1926. Chain plates and deadeyes at the rails await masts and shrouds. Deck hardware is not in place, save for the windlass in the bow. Note the "binnacle peep" in the cabin trunk to the right of the companionway, for the helmsman to view the compass. The donkey engine is in the box ahead of the foremast fife rail. GORDON W. THOMAS COLLECTION

manner when she laid over in a blow, they secured stringers athwartships over the ballast and spiked flooring thereon.

In ballast, *Adventure* looked more comfortable. With the addition of her engine and spars she would settle down on her haunches, ready to spring to life. The engine was a 120-horsepower Fairbanks Morse diesel, bedded and aligned with the shaft to Fred Thomas's satisfaction.

Her spars were impressive enough—Oregon fir that was recently reaching for heaven, now lying down waiting to be restored to the upright. They were beyond doubt shaped at Thurston's, Gloucester's leading spar shed, which was tucked in at the head of Harbor Cove. This haven of shavings was only a five-minute stroll from the Thomas manse. The shaping, tapering, finishing, and slushing-down, and the fitting of the hardware—most of which was beaten out in one of the waterfront blacksmith shops—had been proceeding during the summer while the new schooner was building.

From the lofty shears that were familiar landmarks where such elevating work was still done at a few of the wharves, the riggers raised each mast to the sky, swung it over, and lowered it gingerly through its hole in the deck to its step on the keelson.

Although the measurements are not recorded, *Adventure*'s first mainmast must have been in excess of seventy feet above deck (eighty or more from heel to cap) and nineteen inches in diameter at shoulder height. The foremast was at least sixty feet high from the deck and eighteen inches in diameter. The mast hoops were of ash, steam-bent, copper-riveted, two feet across on the inside, and slipped on *before* the stepping or there was hell to pay.

The main boom was a foot thick and likely around seventy feet long, extending ten feet or so outboard of the taffrail, and the main gaff some forty feet. The fore boom was seven or eight inches in diameter and close to twenty-seven feet long, the gaff the same length though not so heavy. The jumbo boom from the jumbo stay just forward of the windlass was a slight stick of only about fifteen feet, merely enough to knock you overboard if you got in the way of a jibe.

Standing rigging was galvanized wire. Main and fore shrouds were ratlined and set up at the sheerpoles with lanyards and deadeyes from the chainplates. The jumbo stay ran from the pawl post ahead of the windlass to the fore crosstrees, the jibstay from stem to foremasthead. The running rigging was manila and included the main and fore gaff throat and peak halyards, jib and jumbo halyards, pennant halyards, downhauls, outhauls, topping lifts, dory tackles, mainsheet (three and a half inches around), fore sheet, jumbo sheet, and jibsheet.

The sails were of heavy duck, measured, cut, and handstitched by one of the four lofts still operating in Gloucester. The anchor was surely banged out at the noisy Cape Ann Anchor and Forge works next to the railroad drawbridge over the Annisquam River, five or six hundred pounds. Jeff didn't drop his hook unless he had to, and it doesn't seem that he carried a spare.

Adventure carried fourteen double (two-man) dories, probably built by Hiram Lowell in Amesbury, about fourteen feet by close to five feet on the bottom, eighteen feet long on the gunwale. The thwarts were removable so they could be nested on both sides of the deck between the masts and tied down to ringbolts in rough weather. The dory outfits included fifty-six oars and spares, tholepins, masts and sails, bailers, trawl tubs, trawls, anchors, buoys and lines, torches, and compasses.

All this and a thousand more details. Total cost of *Adventure*, ready for sea but minus stores, food, fuel, ice, salt, and bait, was believed by Gordon Thomas to be $65,000—which was big money in those days. He thought his father's was the most expensive schooner yet to sail out of Gloucester, though the earlier *Puritan* surely must have given a ride—and such a short one—for the money.

All this fitting-out, from ballast to baked beans, took but a frenzied three weeks. Exactly a month to the day from her launching, *Adventure* sailed on her maiden trip haddocking. It was October 16, 1926. Six days later Jeff hailed into the Boston Fish Pier with 70,000 pounds. Not a bad start.

Haddocking winters, halibuting summers—that was the way Jeff liked to fish, and he was highline at both. The succulent giant flounder was getting fished out after many generations of kill, and the vessels had to go farther and farther for them, six-week trips sometimes. Weighing into the hundreds of pounds, halibut kept well after they were cleaned and iced down. *Adventure* carried block ice, which the men chipped and jammed into the body cavities and then packed around them.

A formidable creature on a trawl, a big halibut. Captain Felix Hogan had all his dories out from the *L.A. Dunton* one time, all hauling back their trawl but one, way off, with a pair of greenhorns in it, as Leo Hynes tells the story. The rest were almost finished when Felix nosed up alongside the two to see what was keeping them. One was perched way up in the bow, the other in the stern. In between was a monster halibut, flapping around in the bottom, and he'd about cleaned everything out of the dory but his captors. "What in hell's wrong with you fellers?" inquired Captain Hogan. "Jaysus, skipper," yelled one of them, "we got one on the first hook, and warn't he cross!" They were scared half to death and were waiting up in the ends for the old fish to wear himself out.

Such shenanigans didn't bother Jeff's men. They just biffed the big ones on the nose with the killer stick and dragged them in over the gunwale. They celebrated their first year in *Adventure* on October 3, 1927, with a trip of 100,000 pounds of halibut for the Boston market. Stocked $11,700—that's what it sold for—and each man's share was $276, good money then. It was to prove Jeff's biggest fare in *Adventure*. In her first two years, calculated his son, she paid for herself.

There are few first-hand stories of Jeff Thomas. He died fifty years ago, and hardly a soul is left who fished with him. Leo Hynes had one encounter at sea with the man he succeeded and enjoys recalling it. Leo was in his first command, the *Mary O'Hara*, in 1931, the dories getting plenty of fish but on a foul bottom in a fierce tide somewhere on the heel (as opposed to the northeast toe) of Browns Bank.

Along comes *Adventure* with Captain Jeff. "He rounded up on our stern and wanted to know how the fishing was. I was glad to see him, because I was kinda lost. I hailed him. 'Where the hell are we, Cap'n Jeff?' He says, 'Boy, yer away the hell up on the heel o' Browns. I wouldn't set a trawl here for a million bucks!' Well, I was about thirty miles away from where I thought I was. I was lost half the time

Opposite: *Moved to another wharf, the brand new schooner* Adventure *now boasts spars and hoops, standing rigging (shrouds and headstays), and some of her running rigging. The main boom crutch has been set up, but neither main nor fore boom.* Adventure *looks to have her ballast by this time. The exhaust pipe for the original Fairbanks Morse engine is visible in the counter.* GORDON W. THOMAS COLLECTION

in those days. The tide had overhauled me, but the fishing was so damn good we just stayed there anyway and loaded up."

At sea, Jeff kept to himself and could be moody. So his son was told. On one occasion several of the crew were struggling to sheet in the foresail. Jeff watched them for a minute, suddenly charged in, swept them all aside, and hauled it himself—testimony to his impulsiveness and his strength; in his later years he weighed in at 260 pounds.

How he loved to sail! When he had a mind to, and the breeze suited him, according to Harry Eustis, one of the last of the sailing Gloucestermen, Captain Jeff would silently go below, "oil-up" (don his oilskins), get into his Red Jack boots, and reappear on deck. That was the sign for the crew to go and do likewise, because they were in for some excitement. And when he really had her a-goin' full and by, every sail pulling, his special spot was up by the weather break, one arm crooked in the main rigging. There he could keep an eye on everything and everyone, and rejoice to himself in the rush of the green water over his lee rail and the crack of the wind in the canvas above.

For one who had grown up with sail, learned to fish under sail, earned a reputation as one of Gloucester's wilder sail carriers, it must have been a wrenching experience for Jeff Thomas to furl *Adventure*'s mainsail for the last time in his and her fishing career. Just when he did it is in some doubt. In the earliest known photograph of *Adventure*, in the *Atlantic Fisherman* of November 1932, the big gaff mainsail is gone and the leg-o'-mutton riding sail she carried for the next twenty-one years is furled in its place. The change may have been occasioned by the replacement, probably in 1931 or 1932, of the original 120-h.p. Fairbanks Morse diesel with another one of 180. John Flannagan went transient engineer for a couple of trips around that time, when Fred Thomas was ailing, and recalls that the new engine would drive her at a fair turn of speed. Reason enough for a practical man to be forced to concede that his iron topsail was his iron mainsail as well.*

It was a mark of the times, having to admit that before your very eyes engine power was proving superior to sail for consistent speed, maneuverability, convenience, and safety. "That kind of a vessel didn't take much to drive her," said Flannagan. Ample testimony to ample old Tom McManus, the Merlin of the two-masters. "A good sea vessel? Gawd, you had to go up on deck to find out if it was blowin'." And Captain Jeff? "Nice man. Very rugged man. Nothin' seemed to disturb him. Never saw him angry."

Like the buggy-whip holders that former carriage-makers persisted in screw-

---

* In the altered rig, the main riding sail was bent to the hoops up to the crosstrees, the head of it set flying from that point to the masthead. A standing backstay was run from the masthead down to the deck aft of the mainsheet horse, on a tackle for setting it up. The riding sail sheet was rove through the old mainsheet deck block. This backstay stiffened up the rig via the spring- and jibstays to the stem so that the riding sail and its sheet wouldn't take the whole strain when the other lowers were pulling or when *Adventure* plunged into a sea and her masts wanted to lunge.

ing to the first automobile bodies, *Adventure*'s mastheads continued to boast the hardware that Jeff, in what must have been a burst of wishfulness, had ordered for topmasts, which meant topsails and a fisherman staysail—just in case time should happen to turn back.

The next step into comfortable conformity, the excrescence that sealed the fate of the era, was the addition of a pilothouse. Jeff must have had that built with many a shake of the head. It enclosed the wheelbox right up over the cabintop and companionway slide. Of course with the main boom gone, there was headroom enough for such sissy shelter from the storm and the boarding seas and the arctic blast, with doors and peekaboo windows and heat welling up from the engine room. And why not? Why stand out there on a slant in a gale, gripping the deck and the wheel for dear life, stung by spray and up to your hips in water, just because they'd been doing it for three hundred years?

So a wheelhouse it was. Tanny Tanner, skipper in his own right by then, came aboard with his carpenter one day when *Adventure* was in one of the Novie ports and with his old mentor's permission measured up this decadent structure and built one to match on his *Marguerite B. Tanner*, the first Lunenburg schooner to sport such a travesty.

And *Adventure*, how did she take to this plastic surgery, to these further amendments to the purity of her pedigree? Well, she commenced to leak back around the sternpost, where she was told where she was going and where she knew where she'd been. And she began balking at taking the skipper to the fish. As 1933 wore on, it seemed as if their luck, in common with the rest of the world's, was off. Jeff just couldn't seem to lay his dories on the good spots, and he started having crew troubles—good men quitting, being replaced by some not so good.

As for the leak, after almost every trip he had to haul her out, looking for that pesty leak. They ripped off planking around the stern but couldn't put their finger on it. She just kept the whereabouts of that damn leak to herself.

To top it off, Jeff nearly lost the best engineer a man could hope for. Cousin Fred Thomas came down with pneumonia while they were fishing off Nova Scotia in late October, and Jeff had to rush him into the hospital in Halifax in the teeth of a living gale.

That December of the deepening Depression, 1933, they had been fishing around Western and Sable banks, hoping to slip home in time for Christmas, 40,000 pounds of cod and haddock already iced below, when it came on to blow and snow, heavy, and she came on to leak again, bad. It was the twenty-second.

Jeff struck a compass course for Sheet Harbor, Nova Scotia, and put the gang to work at the pumps. Blinding snowstorm now, leaking an inch a minute. Sheet, as he knew too well, was a harbor hard to make under the best of conditions. Narrow entrance between jagged rocks and ledge. He reflected with a grimace. Shades of the winter of 1914, and *Sylvania* up on White Shoal.

*The only known photograph of Adventure during the Jeff Thomas era ran in
the November 1932 Atlantic Fisherman, showing her at a Portland wharf where
she had come in for bait and ice during a halibuting trip. Jeff had swapped
the gaff mainsail and boom for a riding sail, but there is still no pilot house.
The engine stack rises out of the deck aft and to starboard of the mainmast.
Adventure appears to be carrying fourteen dories and therefore a big crew.
The barrels lashed to the rail aft of the cabin may hold extra fuel or possibly
are reserved for liver oil. The Lothrop patented, hand-cranked fog horn,
a Gloucester specialty, sits beside the wheelbox. SHARP COLLECTION*

CAR-RUNCH! *White Shoal*! Right out of the thick and full tilt, *Adventure* bid
up on that selfsame ledge and hung there, the seas crashing all around. Some of the
boys were swinging the dories over to abandon her, but Jeff jumped in among them
and roared them back to the pumps. By God, they were going to save her. Then he
did get one of them in a dory into Sheet Harbor, and a towboat was summoned.

They struck Friday night, late. Pumped like the devil all that night and all day Saturday. Threw the 40,000 pounds of fish and 6,000 of bait overboard to lighten her. A sea jumped the rail and flicked their mascot collie, Peggy, back with it, the only lamented casualty. They pumped Saturday night, all day Sunday, and Sunday night, which was Christmas Eve. Christmas Day they pumped and had haddock chowder to celebrate. The tug *Coalopolis* steamed up and got a hawser aboard, and late Christmas afternoon hauled them off. It was a forty-mile tow to Halifax, pumping all the way to the railway across the harbor at Dartmouth, and then relief, after 104 solid hours of chain-gang labor.

Just as it had done to *Sylvania*, White Shoal had robbed *Adventure* of a long chunk of her keel and her entire rudder. "The *Adventure* is credited as being one of the finest fishing schooners afloat," worried the *Gloucester Times* when the delayed news arrived by telegraph, "and Gloucester can ill afford to lose her."

Twelve days of frustration passed. It was the New Year, 1934, and Jeff Thomas sat down in Halifax on the sixth of January, lonely and weary, to write "Babe," his married elder daughter, Florence Wiley. The patient wife and mother, Lulu, had died in 1928 at only fifty-one.

Dear Babe

I thought it time to write you a few lines to let you know that I am alive and well but that is all I can say. I suppose you heard all kinds of stories of what has happend. Well it has been a preety hard trip all around and it is far from being any better for the trouble is now to get the vessell fixed up and the crew satified. They are demaning money for saving the vessell and insurance wont pay them. So they are after me for it. So you can imagine what kind of a time I am having. Well I suppose I have got to put up with.

I dont know how long we will be here but I think we will be here a week or more. Write me a letter as soon has get this one for a want to know how thing are getting along in regards to money matters and how everybody is.

There was an Insurance Policy due the 24th of Dec. to Jonson's but he will have to wait ontill I get home.

This is I think the hard place on earth to be. We've had the worst kind of weather from snow storns to 10 below zero. You can hardly stand on the streets. I think I wrote all I can think of so will close with love to all.

From your

Father

Another six days passed, and the skipper of the landbound *Adventure* wrote Florence again, on January 12.

Dear Babe

Received your letter this morning and was glad to hear from you. We are still here but hope to get away next week. I have been looking for a Letter since yesterday but never got it untill this morning. Well things are a little better than when I wrote last. The Insurance has made a settlement with the crew so it has made it a little better for me. The weather has been better also. In regards to that check I will indorse it but you will have to get somebody to witness it. The bank will probly not want to give you that much but tell them that you got to have it to pay expenses. You will have to put the number of the book yourself.

Well this has been a vacasun for me. I hope that it will be the last one. There nobody to talk to. Not even the crew would talk to me. In regards to cloase I had some onboard and I sent some to the laundry so I guess I'll get along.

We are going to fit out again and try to get a trip before we get home if things go alright. There is not much to write about. It the same thing over again. You will not get this untill Monday. So you can write again if you want to and if I don't get it it can be returned. We are almost ready to come off the Slip, but there is a lot of engine work to do yet. You will have to make this money go as far has it can go for money is going to be scarce. If things work alright we might be home in a couple of weeks so cheer up it might be worst.

From your

Father

Give everbody my regards.

In fact, it was a couple of weeks before they even got off the railway, a mighty expensive grounding, and only on January 26 did *Adventure* head back for the banks, her men hoping to make up some of the loss from the "broker" incurred when they returned their hard-caught 40,000 pounds perforce to the sea that night on White Shoal. Not until a fortnight later, on February 8, did they hail into Boston, and with only a fair trip, after an absence of eight weeks.

When they arrived, one of the deepest freezes within memory gripped the coast. Gloucester Harbor was so solid that nothing could move in or out, and the townspeople were all over the inner harbor, skating, iceboating, and ice fishing for eels. *Adventure* couldn't get home to the Independent Fisheries wharf for a week. When she finally got through, Jeff told "Squibs," the fishing news columnist for the *Gloucester Times,* that he'd probably make a few more trips haddocking before calling it quits and refitting for fresh halibuting. They baited and iced and were off again on February 17, when the harbor ice was broken momentarily by the Coast Guard with the help of a wind shift.

More bad luck. Jeff couldn't lay his dories on the haddock. They were coming in with codfish, and with rock-bottom prices in prospect, he headed home in some disgust. Bound in for Boston on February 27, they were only forty-five miles off Eastern Point when they broke down. Jeff put out a distress call, and the Coast Guard patrol boat *Frederick Lee* steamed out from Gloucester, where it had been breaking more ice, and towed them to Boston, where they sold their trip, such as it was. Then another tow—not for free this time—and back on the railway at Gloucester. *Adventure* had lost her propeller, according to one report—her rudder, according to another. Maybe both if the wheel spun off the shaft and took the rudder with it.

How Highliner Jeff must have squirmed when, after three more precious and costly weeks of repairs, Squibs offered this backhanded condolence in the *Times*: "The crew of sch. *Adventure*, Capt. Jeff Thomas, are reported as faring rather poorly

The naval architect and historian Howard I. Chapelle inspected Adventure in some detail when she was hauled out in 1934. D. FOSTER TAYLOR COLLECTION, PEABODY MUSEUM OF SALEM

on their last trip, when Squibs heard the crew shared but $12 each. Tough luck and then some!"

And then there was the drinking.

When did it start, and why? After he lost the two astray from the *Benjamin Smith* in 1920? Or the blow of the *Puritan* and Chris Johnson's drowning in 1922? Brother Billy died of a heart attack in 1925. Lulu died so prematurely in 1928. Brother Freeman suffered a heart attack and expired in his bunk aboard *Adventure* in 1931. And these recent reverses. There is evidence, on the other hand, that one does not "turn to drink" unless one is so predisposed.

"They said he could hold his liquor better than any man in Gloucester," Gordon Thomas reflected fifty years later. "At home, he'd get up in the morning, cook himself a big meal—steak, several eggs, home fries—put that under his belt, and down the street to meet the other skippers and make the rounds all day and come home to Washington Square and walk a straight line. The liquor he put away that day! And he could hold it.

"There was only one time. A snowstorm. Mother was sitting in the window looking for him. And she saw him coming, but he disappeared. She sent me down, and I found him in a snowbank, his feet sticking out.

"He was very jolly when he got a few under his belt, very generous, never abused anybody, never put a hand on one of us. And when he went to sea, that was the end of it. No drinking."

Cooling his heels on his enforced holiday vacation in Halifax, Jeff grew despondent and was drinking pretty heavily, so heavily, said Gordon, that when they did get back to Gloucester, his father was in such bad shape that it scared him off the bottle.

And then the breakdown. More costly repairs, more costly lay days on the railway, more missed fishing, and on March 21, 1934, *Adventure* finally left Boston for Western Bank again, haddocking, eighty miles off Halifax.

In three days, on March 24, they were on the grounds, and the skipper put the dories over for the first set. It had been bitterly cold on the way up, smashing into head seas, and everywhere the spray hit, it froze.

Adventure was sheathed in ice, logy and top-heavy, so while the boys were out setting, and she jogged along, Jeff went to work, as he had hundreds of times before on dozens of vessels, whacking away at it with whatever came to hand to lighten her up and free the frozen gear.

Then he stepped into the pilothouse to take the wheel and change his course just a hair—and collapsed on the deck and died. He had just turned fifty-nine.

The dories came in, and his men packed Captain Jeff in ice and sailed into Halifax and sent him home to Gloucester.

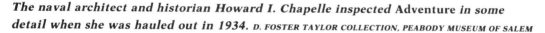

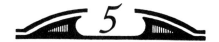

Leo
the Lighthearted

We had a bunch of really tough fellers up there in the fo'c'sle.
Of course, I was very timid.

Leo Hynes

eo Hynes was born in the fishing village of Bay l'Argent, way up on the eastern shore of Fortune Bay along the south coast of Newfoundland, August 12, 1900, under the sign of Leo. So it was his manifest destiny to be a lion among those who go down to the sea, a great fisher of *l'argent de la mer*, and an uncommon mariner and a fortunate one, making his appearance at the turn of the century astride the old and the new of his inherited calling.

Besides the presiding stars, his father and mother had something to do with his arrival, as they did with the lighthearted side of him and the lionhearted, Patrick Hynes being of the Irish and Margaret West of the English.

Like a glacial colossus, the formidable island of Newfoundland guards the entrance to the Gulf of St. Lawrence between Nova Scotia's Cape Breton Island and Labrador. The island's interior is wilderness, the coast not much better, fog-dogged and, until recent years, nigh roadless. Such a hard place is fit only for that tough race of fishermen and their families who for centuries have clung to the raw edge of the ocean, wresting their small schooners from the forest and with them a lean living from the sea. Fortune Bay on the south coast, scantily protected from the easterlies by the Burin Peninsula, has long been for "the Boston states" an ever-renewable source of master mariners after their fortunes elsewhere, for there was none to be made at home, for all the name of it.

Leo's father owned and fished what was called a jack schooner, or jack boat—characterized by a broad stern and outboard rudder—out of Bay l'Argent. His father's father had three of them. The boy stayed with his mother's parents across the harbor for seven winters, however, because the school was better there. Summers he went saltfishing around the coast in the Strait of Belle Isle between Newfoundland and Labrador. At sixteen he started dory trawling in larger schooners, practically around the clock and mighty hard work, from Grand Bank, a town fifty miles farther out on the peninsula.

About due west of Burin lie the barren islands of St. Pierre and Miquelon, the base of the French cod fishery. The smaller St. Pierre is the capital. Besides fishing, the sly *pêcheurs* of St. Pierre et Miquelon were heirs to a perfunctorily legal and profoundly profitable tradition of catering to any and all smugglers of spirituous liquors, be they Canadian or, when Prohibition became the silliest law of the land in January 1920, American. The volume of unilateral commerce between the mainland and the foggy islands belied their size, when you could make them out at all, and the young bucks of Burin considered it their patriotic charge, if the occasion should arise or be made to arise, to embark upon token redress of the balance of payments. Rum was usually the inspiration, the means, or the end of these expeditions—frequently all three.

Our lighthearted young lion and his friends were out fishing on one such occasion and had to anchor in a gale of wind. When they couldn't break it loose, they were forced to cut their cable, no small loss. So they sailed into St. Pierre for a breather, dropped over the spare anchor, and had a good crack at the rum ashore. Leo remembers it well.

"There were a lot of French dory trawlers in there at the time, and we saw this big pile of cable laying on the wharf, all coiled down nice and neat as could be. Apparently going on board of one of the fishermen in the morning. The skipper says, 'By God, we're going to get that cable.'

"So we went back on board the vessel and ran a line ashore and bent it on the end of that cable real quiet, 'cause there were Frenchmen all around on the dock. Got back on board and set the mainsail, hove the anchor up and set the foresail and the headsails. Nice breeze, and we struck off down the harbor at a good clip.

"Those Frenchmen didn't know what was happening. We saw a bunch of them jump for that cable as it went whistling off the dock, but they couldn't hold it, not a chance! We sailed halfway to Grand Bank, hove to and put the cable on

Leo Hynes, a few days short of his thirtieth birthday, was doubtless single-dory trawling in the schooner Commonwealth *when this aerial photograph was taken of her home base, the Boston Fish Pier, on July 24, 1930. Built in 1914 off the South Boston waterfront, the pier is surrounded by dory-trawling schooners, beam trawlers, and a few seiners.* Adventure *generally berthed along the right-hand side across from Commonwealth Pier, where a Luckenbach freighter is unloading cargo. Co-owner Phil Manta's grocery and chandlery is on Northern Avenue behind the Fish Pier.* FAIRCHILD AERIAL SURVEYS, INC.

the windlass and cranked it all in. I still remember the expressions on those Frenchmen trying to stop that cable whistling out to sea."

All in good fun, of course; the Newfies would go to any lengths to pull a fast one on the Frenchmen.

Around this time the young lion had saved a few hundred dollars, and he convinced his father (who was reluctant at first but who the son doubts ever made more than three hundred a year fishing in his life) to take him in the jack schooner across the strait to St. Pierre, fill her up with rum at the going rate of fifty cents a bottle, and make a smart dollar retailing the stuff, without the trouble of duty, back home. So they did, and Leo bought a batch of cigars for his old man and coffee for his mother.

"Back in those days they had a slow old steam Coast Guard cutter, and she would belch volumes of black smoke. We had barely set our course for home when my father says, 'There it is! There's the cutter! They're going to take my boat, put me in jail, and we'll lose everything, by God!'

"The cutter was on the horizon and steaming along as fast as she could bang those old pistons of hers. We decided there was nothing to do but hide behind the high land of the island, so we sailed around to the back side and hove to til dark. Then we made a run for it and got home all right, and tied up, and took all that rum ashore and buried it in the field next to the house. My father never rested that night til he shoveled the last dirt on top of that load of booze.

"Next day we called the customs man and told him we were home, and he came down to clear us and sign us in, and then up to the house for a cup of tea. My mother knew what was going on, but when she saw us walk in with the customs she about went through the floor. Thought we'd been caught and were on our way to jail. She kept her composure, though, all through the tea, and then confessed her fears to us."

Ma Hynes didn't know the half of it. The warehouses over on St. Pierre were built down on the wharves, out over the water, and in one of them they stored rum in great casks six feet across. Her son was out fishing one time when a gale arose, and they put in to St. Pierre for shelter. Idled heads soon turned to mischief. They scrubbed out a dory and dropped it overboard in the dead of night, and then another. Then they slipped into the second and silently towed the first in under the rum wharf.

"We took a big auger with us, and we had to bore several holes up through the floor before we finally struck one of those casks. But when we did, my God didn't the rum flow! We filled the dory up in no time. It was still running strong when we had to get out of there for fear of swamping the boat. We rowed back and filled everything we had aboard the schooner, pots, pans, everything we could lay our hands on, and we still had to throw a lot of it away. Hoisted the dory aboard a quarter full. I wonder if those Frenchmen ever found out what happened to their rum."

The young lion was around sixteen when he decided that there had to be something better than fishing out of Newfoundland, so he talked himself into a berth on one of the old three-masted tern schooners freighting salt fish to Portugal and Spain, a trade that boomed briefly during World War I. The fish was cured down on the beaches by the women of Grand Bank, who were paid twenty-five cents a quintal of 112 pounds.

During one crossing the skipper made the mistake of sailing straight into the Sargasso Sea in the North Atlantic, where they were becalmed for a week in that infamous vortex of seaweed, marine life, and ocean debris. Tiny crabs crawled up the sides and all over the deck. The crew let the sails down and painted and tidied up until a little breeze finally sprang up from nowhere and wafted them out of the strange stagnation.

Now and then the Newfie saltbankers would turn to coasting in the fall of the year, and it was on one of these trips to Boston for a cargo of flour, only six men in the crew and no power, that Leo Hynes was signed on as mate by the skipper, who proved to be in his first command. It breezed up right sharp one night, and they were taking in the mainsail and trying to crutch the main boom when it got away from them and knocked a man overboard.

"We launched a dory. The cook and I jumped in and rowed back. We could hear the feller scream but couldn't find him in the dark and stayed a little bit too long. The vessel still had foresail and jumbo up, and the skipper was all upset and didn't know enough to jibe her over. He didn't know where we were, and we didn't have a light, and she was joggin' along so fast, must have taken us an hour, both of us rowing, to catch up. We almost lost our lives that night. The poor feller in the water, that was the end of him."

Leo was an affable young bruiser, ever on the lookout to learn more of the ways of the world. On occasion he learned more than he wanted to know. It happened that he was in Boston in the Prohibition spring of 1923 in the saltbanker *Maud Thornhill* with a short cargo of salt herring, their 86-proof liquor lading having been more profitably disposed of on Rum Row at the outer edge of the three-mile limit.

Returning, they found their home coast blocked by drift ice and so put into Halifax. Tied up there, and shorthanded, was the small Novie schooner *Eddie James* of Yarmouth, which had just suffered the insult of a hijacking off New Jersey. Five bully boys from a powerful steamer had pulled up and boarded behind a volley of gunfire that wounded the supercargo, then proceeded in leisurely fashion to relieve the rumrunners of the unsold remainder of their six hundred cases and eight grand in cash.*

The captain of the *Eddie James* was offering a hundred dollars a month and a hundred bonus when the booze was sold—good money—and Leo signed on. She had just been rerigged but had no power. They sailed to St. Pierre for the hooch, which the skipper sampled liberally, to be sure of its quality, as they shaped a course for New York. Then he issued guns all around, and it breezed up to a living gale.

"He had us all scared half to death, 'cause he was half loaded, and we were just young fellers, and it was blowing fifty knots. We were still carrying a whole mainsail. We had a man lashed to the wheel, standing on a caribou skin nailed to the deck to keep his feet warm. We had set up the rigging when we sailed, but with the seas running out there, the masts cavorting around up aloft, it slacked off

---

* And a grim aftermath, if aftermath it was. The 150-foot steamer *John Dwight* out of Newport was encountered by the Coast Guard in Vineyard Sound in the fog, decks awash. Before their eyes, she rolled over, her boilers exploded, and she sank. No survivors. Next day eight bodies in life preservers, battered as if in a battle, were plucked out of the Sound amid barrels of ale. There were no answers, only theories.

considerable. So we had to get on the lee side and set it up when we were on one tack, and set it up on the other side when we were on the other tack, standing in water chest high in the lee scuppers when she'd roll.

"The old man finally decided to take in the mainsail, the vessel fairly leaping along, and we'd just dropped it—we were all lashed to the pinrails—when a great big wave come over, and one man started screaming his head off, fighting, sounded

Everything flying but the cook's undershirt, the racing fisherman Gertrude L. Thebaud *struts her stuff off Gloucester in a brisk sou'wester that fills her canvas with wind and beauty. From the fresh look of her, the photograph was taken soon after her launching in 1930. A gang of guests hugs the weather bulwarks. When Captain Leo Hynes had her fishing out of Gloucester before he took* Adventure, *the* Thebaud *had changed her yachting gown for the workaday duds of a dirty dory trawler.* ADOLPH KUPSINEL PHOTO, AUTHOR'S COLLECTION

as though he was dying. Well, come to find out, that caribou skin had washed off the deck and landed on him, and he couldn't see nothing, this big furry thing covering his head completely, and he panicked.

"We got up off New York, outside the limit, and the boats came along to buy, but the skipper would say, 'Our cargo is consigned. Don't come near us or you'll be shot!' We were waiting for someone to come out with a blue light. Each night he'd tell us, 'If anybody tries to board, shoot him!' We had a couple of steel shields up around the windlass. I had a double-barreled shotgun. I was scared to death. I says to myself, 'I don't want to murder anybody, and I don't want to get shot. If I ever get off this rumrunner I'm never gonna get aboard of another one.' "

The *Eddie James* was off New York for a month selling her cargo. Almost home to Yarmouth, the boys still didn't have their money—and they wondered if they were going to get it. So they had a little rump session up forward, trooped back up on deck, brought the *Eddie James* into the wind, and informed the skipper that that was that until they were paid off. They were.

Just to protect themselves, en route to New York they had been sneaking into the fishhold and sneaking out a certain cut of the consignment. They hid the bottles here and there, such as under a mattress in a bunk, which after a while rose so high a man could hardly sleep on it, and so lumpy it nearly threw him on the floor when she rolled. They knew they could get a good price for it back home. But their skipper outfoxed them.

"When we got into Yarmouth and tied up, the old man came down with the owner, and he says, 'Listen, fellers, if you have any booze in here you better not touch it, 'cause the customs boys are watching us and they're coming to take it all. They're getting very strict and will go over the vessel and all your gear with a fine-tooth comb!'

"So we got scared and left it all aboard. We heard afterward that the old man sold every drop of it and made a mint. I don't think there were any customs boys within a hundred miles. But we must have had twelve cases in the forward peak alone."

If not rumrunning, then what? For a dollar a day the young lion signed on an aged coasting schooner bound for New York with lumber, returning with coal. When they reached New York, three of them, including the mate, who was probably making two dollars a day, took off for Boston. To get past Immigration, aliens then had to show they had a hundred dollars. Leon had only fourteen, but among them they got it up. First one went through with the hundred, and then another, slipping it back to the next for recycling.

In Boston the Newfies found a room for twelve dollars a week on lower Tremont Street. *Abie's Irish Rose* was playing nearby in the Castle Square Theatre. Their elderly landlady took a liking to the lighthearted one and found him a job moving furniture. But they didn't have enough left among them to pay the rent and

The earliest photo of Adventure *under way, in 1937, shows her leaving Gloucester. The Rockaway Hotel on Rocky Neck is in the dim background just ahead of the rather recent pilot house. This is about how she looked when she came to Leo Hynes in 1934. Her rig is unaltered since her sailing days, except for the main riding sail. Main peak halyard bands have been stripped of their blocks, but the topmast hardware wistfully installed by Captain Jeff is still up there.* GORDON W. THOMAS COLLECTION

departed in the early hours one morning, intending to come back some time and pay her, but they never quite got around to it.

Unable to make more than twenty-two a week, Leo signed on the bulk carrier *Mars*, about eight thousand tons, bound for Norfolk. Six months later they were caught in a hurricane off Cuba's Daiquiri Bay, near Guantanamo, and were wrecked. Hynes and the rest of the crew, except one man who drowned, made it ashore by breeches buoy, and after some wandering about, they hopped a steamer back to New York.

After more kicking around in the merchant marine and some odd-jobbing ashore, the big boy from Bay l'Argent concluded that maybe he could do better fishing, so he drifted down to the Boston Fish Pier and a site in the schooner *Hortense*, one of the big O'Hara Brothers fleet, fresh halibuting. It was to be the last time he would go fishing wholly under sail—sail alone because her two old engines were broken down most of the time. They were gone seven weeks dory trawling, and his share was fourteen dollars, two bucks a week. So he found a job in a factory in Somerville, a Boston suburb.

But the old bug had bitten. A friend had gone up to Gloucester to try it there, with the result that Leo received a call from Captain Ivor Carlson looking for a man to go halibuting in Gorton-Pew's auxiliary schooner *Acushla*. This was around 1925. Then in the *Hesperus* and then back to Boston in the big new haddocker *Lark*, built in Newcastle, Maine, in 1922 by the O'Haras for Captain Ernest Parsons, who was on the road to fame as a highliner. Next came a few winter trips in Gloucester's sentimental old favorite, *Elsie*, with Captain Morton L. Selig.*

And then another bug bit, and Leo Hynes and Lillian Banfield, his childhood sweetheart from Bay l'Argent, were married on December 6, 1927. Lil first arrived in the States when she was seventeen simply by strolling across the bridge from New Brunswick to Calais, Maine, one night. Somebody told her that wasn't official enough, so a few years later she got around to reentering Canada and came back again by the light of day, making it so.

There was some strained feeling between the Catholic and Protestant families back in their native village, and when Lil's friends heard of her marriage to one of the former, they exclaimed: "What! Of all the men in the United States, you had to pick Leo Hynes?"

From the *Lark*, Leo bounced to the fo'c'sle of Captain Parsons's chief rival out of Boston, Captain Frank Watts in the schooner *Commonwealth*, single-dory trawling. Single-dorying, a man to a dory with twenty-two or twenty-four dories out, covered more territory, farther and harder to row and harder to haul, and was about twice as hard as double-dorying. Leo knew; he had gone single-dorying back home.

One of *Commonwealth*'s crew was John Buller from Newfoundland, an old bachelor who was in his cups most of the time and wet outside, too—because he dressed in rags and rubber boots with holes in them. Somebody asked him once if he could swim, and he snapped, "Nope, and it's no sense when it's sixty miles from land. Who's gonna swim that far? Besides, I'm a doryman and there's always a boat around somewhere."

They were single-dorying on Georges, thick o' fog, and John Buller went astray. They heard the story later. A steamer eased up alongside and the captain yelled down, did he want to be picked up?

"Well, where you going, Cap?"

---

* Three years after she was overwhelmed by *Bluenose* in the 1921 races, *Elsie* received a 100-h.p. engine, hardly enough to more than help her along under sail in light airs. *Elsie* was the first command of Mort Selig, who went on to be a highliner beam trawling. In 1984 Captain Selig was still a familiar figure as Gloucester's senior master mariner—erect as a ramrod, driving his car and shopping for groceries at the age of ninety-five.

"We're going to New York."

"Oh, well, give me a little grub. I want to go to Boston, and I'll just keep rowin'."

Either that, or there was another boat around somewhere.

The Novie port of Shelburne used to put on some pretty wild dances for the fishermen who had taken refuge during a blow, or had come in for ice or bait, and *Commonwealth* put in there one winter night—the cold was something fierce—and the gang walked up to the dance. Leo had a pop bottle of red rum in his back pocket. They had pulled the shades in the place. He was swinging this old girl around and around, a pretty heavy old girl, and they swung right through the window and into a snowbank—shade, glass, and all.

Back inside, the evening danced on.

"Old Jim Morash was the engineer, a long-sparred feller that stood six foot four, and I gave him my pop bottle and he guzzled it and sank right down in the corner. Well, it was some cold. We went back aboard the vessel, and the next morning Jim was missing. We come in looking for him, and he's out sitting on the doorstep where the dance was, and it's about twenty below and still blowing.

" 'My God, Jim, how come you're not inside?'

" 'Wal, the cat froze on the chair, an' I figgered 'twas warmer outside.' "

By 1931 Leo and Lil had two boys, young Leo and newborn Al. The Depression was settling in, and although the breadwinner had a regular site with the O'Hara schooner *Gossoon* out of Boston, the outlook for the Hynes family was bleak. But then came the big break. The regular skipper of their schooner *Mary E. O'Hara* went home to Nova Scotia for the winter, and Pat O'Hara asked Leo if he would take her. He was thirty-one and ready, and he didn't have to be asked twice.

Pat O'Hara was a bit of a wit. Back at the Boston Fish Pier with his first trip, a whopping 106,000 pounds, Leo wondered what kind of price they could expect. "He asked me if I ever heard of deuces wild. That was it, two cents a pound. The crew shared twenty-one dollars. Mine was a hundred.

"Pat had three sizes of dories on board, and you had to wait for the biggest to come alongside so they'd nest in each other when you got 'em up. I said, 'Pat, can't you give us a set that'll fit?' And he said, 'For God's sake, Leo, next thing you'll want fur-lined dories!' "

The young lion was bound they'd fish over Christmas, not the most popular move he could have made. They were way out on the Grand Bank in the *Mary E.* when the holiday arrived, and he relented, so they ducked into Shelburne and rowed ashore for the dance. About eleven that night they tore themselves away and rowed back out, and she was aground. The rest of the fleet had watched the tide and up-anchored and gone fishing.

"I was some embarrassed, a new skipper, being there in the mud. We finally got off about two in the morning. And where could a feller go then to get a trip of fish? It was so late we decided just to go outside along the shore, inside the three-mile limit. Nobody ever thought of fishing there. But my God, there was plenty of fish! So we stayed there for two days, near Cape Negro.

"And lobsters. The tide had slacked and the buoys were up. The dories were over. There was fog, and I was afraid it would lift and someone would see us and report us to the lighthouse. But we got lobster for the whole gang. Rebaited their pots, of course. And about 70,000 pounds of fish, and went home. The other fellers who went off from the dance early and fished offshore didn't do nearly as well. I was crazy in those days, kinda young I guess, 'cause that was poaching."

When her regular skipper returned to the *Mary E. O'Hara* in 1932, the now-Captain Hynes was invited by Ben Pine, who came from Belleoram, across Fortune Bay from Leo's birthplace, to take the schooner *Ruth and Margaret*, almost twenty years old, dory trawling out of Gloucester for his Atlantic Supply Company.

At about this time—it is not exactly clear when—Piney gave Hynes his pride, the *Gertrude L. Thebaud*, for a few trips, probably as transient for her regular skipper, Jimmy Abbott. The *Thebaud*, the last full-rigged schooner in the fisheries, was built in 1930 by Arthur D. Story in Essex, with high hopes that she would bring the international cup back. She actually defeated *Bluenose* two straight races in October 1933 off Gloucester, though the trophy was not at stake—as it was the next year when she sailed to Halifax and was trounced.

Leo wasn't too happy with the famous flyer as a working vessel. They fished primarily under power, and were underpowered at that, and he felt she was too lively for coming up on the dories, while her tall spars were a disadvantage in a seaway.

Briefly, around this time, he had Jeff Thomas's former command, the *Corinthian*, for Gorton-Pew. Meanwhile, the master of the *Mary E. O'Hara* had sold out his interest in her, and Leo took her out of Boston again for the O'Haras.* It was by now late 1933.

When Captain Jeff died in the pilothouse of *Adventure* on March 24, 1934, Emory Doane, his long-time bos'n, assumed command and took the body of his skipper into Halifax for shipment back to Gloucester. And then they returned to the banks, as Jeff would have wanted, finished the trip, and sailed to Boston.

Jeff's son, Gordon, took the train to Boston from Gloucester to join Doane and the crew for the sad run home. Off Winthrop her engine blew a piston, as if

---

* The *Mary E. O'Hara* met a ghastly end in the early morning of January 21, 1941, under Captain Fred Wilson. Heavily iced from a gale while coming in, and carrying 50,000 pounds of fish, she ran into a coal barge only three miles from the Boston Fish Pier and sank in shoal water. Eighteen crew drowned or froze to death. Five climbed up in the masts and were rescued after dawn, terribly frostbitten, by a passing beam trawler.

Adventure were reluctant to admit the reality. They raised the distress flag, and in a while the 27,000-ton Cunard liner *Britannic*, just departing Boston, loomed up alongside and hailed them from the bridge through a megaphone. They requested a tug. *Britannic* relayed the message and steamed on for Europe. In due course a towboat hove up and hauled the disabled schooner dejectedly back to Boston for more repairs.

Three weeks later, on April 21, 1934, Squibs passed the rumor in the *Gloucester Times*: "They tell Squibs that Capt. Leo Hines, formerly with the schooner *Mary O'Hara*, which craft he brought into port recently with a big trip, may take over command of sch. *Adventure*."

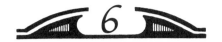

The Compleat Angler

As no man is born an artist, so no man is born an angler.

Izaak Walton
The Compleat Angler

Leo Hynes substantiated the conjectures of Squibs and on the invitation of part-owner Phil Manta, the Boston ship chandler, moved into the main cabin of the schooner *Adventure* on April 28, 1934, for their first trip together, master and vessel. He was thirty-three.

Manta was a small man from a Provincetown family of Portuguese fishermen who never went to sea himself. He gave *Adventure*'s second skipper a sixteenth share (the first of several), his friendship, and his loyalty. Having married in middle life, he treated Leo and Lil like two of his own.

Hynes took aboard his right-hand man, Tom Bambury, who had been with him frequently since they first met as hands on the three-masted schooner *General Currie* of Grand Bank, Newfoundland, in 1919, the year after she was built. That voyage took them forty-seven days on the return from Lisbon—a pleasure cruise compared to a later crossing to Portugal, sixty days and nights against gales and contrary winds that even their cargo of salt fish couldn't stand, and spoiled. And the *General Currie* wasn't much bigger than *Adventure*. Tom Bambury was from

62　*The Compleat Angler*

Fortune Bay, steady as they come, and his friend trusted him with everything, including his life.

Fred Thomas was fifty-two now, much too set in his ways to change. He just naturally came with the schooner whose engines he'd coaxed along for all of her eight years. The new captain was soon boasting of his predecessor's cousin that "Fred knows his engine better than he knows himself. He talks to it, and it purrs right back to him."

After getting her popped piston back purring in Boston, *Adventure* steamed up to Gloucester for refit. While she was hauled out, some of the crew "attended"—as diplomatically phrased by Henry Abbott, who had sailed with the new captain and was there—a big dance "and we raised a little hell, tore down a fence, we were having such fun, but didn't hurt it much." Thus were celebrated the good things that were surely going to occur under the sign of Leo.

Captain Hynes's maiden trip in the dory trawler *Adventure* was both portentous and momentous. They were gone a week and hailed into the Boston Fish Pier on May 4 with 80,000 pounds of haddock, 48,000 of cod, and 12,000 of mixed fish—140,000 pounds, which made them highline haddockers for the fleet.

A hard driver from the hour he took the helm, Leo soon replaced the upright with a concert grand: the 180-horsepower Fairbanks Morse diesel engine with a Cooper-Bessemer of 230 horses. Now Fred Thomas had a friend indeed to talk to, and it purred right back at nine knots.

The new old man made his mark right from the start. Christmas was no more of a time than any for Leo Hynes to be home by the fireside hanging stockings in the middle of the Depression when it was the fish out there that filled them. Five days before Christmas of 1934, a sixty-mile southeast gale swept the Nova Scotia banks, visiting holiday havoc upon the fleet. *Adventure* scudded into Shelburne with three dories smashed on deck. Four weeks later, on their next trip, the rudder broke adrift again off Cape Sable, and they maneuvered back to Shelburne for more repairs, steering, like the chambered nautilus, by the set of their sails.*

Hynes was a driver and a driven man, something inside him always pushing, pushing, pushing.

"I had to make market with a trip of fish. Plenty of nights coming home in

---

* Had it not been for the expensive accident to the rudder, Phil Manta reported to the shareholders, *Adventure* would have turned a profit for 1935, Leo's first full year with her. Thirty-one trips netted $74,251, of which the vessel's share, after paying off the crew, was $16,640. Expenses included the vessel's for the year, $9,434, $3,137 for insurance, and $3,326 for "captain's skippership."

Opposite: *Preparing to sail,* Adventure *takes on crushed ice in fish baskets under Leo Romaine's direction. Cook has his fire going. The swordfish pulpit on the stem has been hauled up out of the way.* JOHN CLAYTON PHOTO

Leo Romaine swings frozen herring aboard for bait. JOHN CLAYTON PHOTO

the wintertime, snowing, gale of wind, we'd run out a southeaster—they'd never last more than twelve hours—take advantage of the fair wind and get as far to the west'ard as we could before it came around nor'west and ahead. But just because it was blowing nor'west I couldn't slow down. We'd go as fast as we could and hope for the best. Storm after storm I'd never turn in. I'd lay on the floor in my oilskins so I'd be ready at a moment's notice.

"Sometimes, driving for the west'ard into hard seas with a hold full of fish, the crew would say, 'You better slow down, skipper.' I'd say, 'What's wrong?' They'd say, 'The beams are moving around in the fo'c'sle.' One of the men in the top bunk said he was scared to put his foot up against the beam for fear one of the knees would pinch his toe. I'd go forward and look around. I'd think I ought to slow down, but I had to make the market. I'd try to pretend there was nothing wrong and go to my bunk and pull the blankets up over my head and pray to God all would hold together."

The time came when he had to wonder seriously how much longer this supervessel he had inherited could take the pounding. The punishment that long, overhanging knockabout bow absorbed from head seas under the power of the new engine, trip after trip, was literally working the oakum out of the seams. And the incurable, infuriating leak down aft somewhere was part of his inheritance. Nor had Jeff helped matters when he damn near wrecked her on that ledge at Sheet Harbor—nor had the farmers that they let loose on her at the Dartmouth shipyard.

It was during one of *Adventure*'s clocklike haulouts at Gloucester that Owen Lantz, the yard foreman, a former master builder of schooners at Essex and Gloucester who was now just keeping his hand in, undertook the unusual measure of jacking up all 250 tons of her on her bilges. And when she rose ever so slowly off the long cradle, her keel just stayed behind, and her garboards too—you could have read the headlines of a newspaper through the gap. Only the buoyancy of the keel pressing up against the floors had been keeping *Adventure* from filling and sinking like a stone.

Wise old Owen Lantz ran new bolts clear down through and drew the errant keel back up where it belonged. To stiffen her backbone and her gyrating bow, he wedded a heavy hunk of oak bracing to her stem piece inside, ahead of the fo'c'sle.

Left: *The luxurious appointments of* Adventure*'s dories include keg buoy and line, trawl anchor, wooden thole pins for rowing (hanging inside the gunwales), kid board to make a fish pen, mast and sail, and plug strap to hang on to if she capsizes. The plug pulls out to drain her when she's safe back aboard.* JOHN CLAYTON PHOTO
Right: *Another luxury allowed the doryman is the nipper, which comes in various guises, here as a grooved band of hard rubber with a knit wool cover demonstrated by Peter Meuse. Makes hauling trawl in a pitching sea a cinch.* JOHN CLAYTON PHOTO

The Compleat Angler 65

And that finally put a stop to the gripes about undue duty at the pumps and the danger of pinched toes in the bunks.

Leo Hynes was among the most successful of all the dory fishermen of his or any other time, and he was the very last, practicing to the limit of human endurance a primeval art already distanced, and in one generation since, nigh forgotten if not lost entirely. What were the elements of this classic pursuit in the twilight of its day?

Ironic it is that the innovations that overtook commercial fishing in the North Atlantic from *Adventure*'s launching in 1926 until her premature retirement in 1953 all stopped short of the dories, so her dorymen kept doggedly on in exactly the old methods they had inherited—every bit as hard, harrowing, and hazardous as they had always been. Auxiliary power, the radio direction finder, the radiotelephone, the fathometer, and Loran—all came to the aid of the skipper and his ability to find fish and drop his dories on them. But the dories, the oars, the trawls, the stoic strength, the hardship, the lurking danger in darkness, fog, and storm—in short, the fishing and the men—were not affected one whit by the changes all about them.

A proud calling, and so it expired. Old age, not a fall, caught up with the proud ones, and they had no successors.

First, there must be bait and ice, the procurement of which was among the myriad of the owner-skipper's shoreside responsibilities in the brief respite between trips—along with paying off the crew's shares, collecting receipts, meeting bills, ordering supplies, overseeing maintenance, keeping an eye on the health of the men, signing on replacements or transients, bailing the drunks out of jail, and trying to bank the home fires. The last was too often the last. On one stretch, Leo had thirteen straight trips without once touching home base (he did snatch a cup of coffee with Lil when she came down to the Fish Pier), and one year, about 1943, *Adventure* made forty-eight trips in a row. It was that kind of driving that earned him the nickname around the fleet of "In-and-Out Hynes."

Squid was the bait favored by fish and fisher. Tough and tasty and it stayed on the hook. Herring was next, cut up in pieces. Mackerel was last because it turned mushy in a couple of days and pulled off the hook. Much of *Adventure*'s bait was trucked frozen from Provincetown. Frozen herring and squid originated in the Nova

Opposite, top: *Done hauling, the dorymen return. One tosses up the painter as he and his mate get set to unload. An incoming dory drops the peak of its sail, and in a few seconds they will have the mast down and the oars out. Engineer Fred Thomas, back to, stands by.* JOHN CLAYTON PHOTO
Bottom: *Mast and sail dropped in the stern, another dory makes it home under the eye of Fred Thomas.* JOHN CLAYTON PHOTO

Scotia and Newfoundland bait fisheries. In the summer *Adventure* would sail with about twelve thousand pounds of frozen bait, a thousand per dory; this would last four days, and if they ran out and were up that way, they would have to run into Novie and hope the rest of the fleet hadn't beaten them to it. It had long since been observed that bait had to be indigenous to the fishing waters; Leo tried West Coast stuff once, and the East Coast fish wouldn't touch it.

As a rule *Adventure* pulled away from the Boston Fish Pier with thirty tons of crushed ice (at five dollars a ton in those days), which left three or four pens in the fishhold for the first of the catch. Only the fresh halibuters and swordfishermen carried block ice, which lasted longer but had to be chipped in the hold as needed. Hynes never took *Adventure* salt fishing.

The hour of departure had less to do with the weather than with the projected hour of arrival on the grounds as determined by the tide table. It was no good to get the trawls caught in a slack tide, when the swinging of the current, which might

From head to toe, the hard life is engraved on the man in the bow. The mast goes through the hole in the thwart behind him. Note the trawl roller on the schooner's rail at far right. JOHN CLAYTON PHOTO

run three or four knots in the opposite direction, would snag and frequently part them. Steaming at nine knots with the assistance of the sails (the Cooper-Bessemer could push her at 9¼ knots in smooth seas), fourteen hours had to be allowed from the Boston Lightship* to the Great South Channel between Nantucket Shoals and the southwest shoals of Georges Bank or the Cultivator Shoal on northwest Georges, a full twenty-four hours to Browns Bank, fifty to Sable Island Bank and nearly three days to the Grand Bank, rarely undertaken.

Before the general advent of electronic aids around the time of World War II, *Adventure* followed ocean pathways well worn by her predecessors. The waters were accurately charted, compass courses memorized, tidal currents predictable and allowed for, the winds vagrant but sniffed in advance by the knowing skipper. The vessel's speeds at such-and-such revolutions of the screw per minute were known quantities. The taffrail log trailing over the stern and beyond the wake did the rest; this was a small, elongated propeller on a length of clothesline that twirled and ticked off, on a gauge at the rail, the distance sailed through the water.

In reality, apparent and actual distance sailed rarely coincided; tidal currents could set you along farther than you thought you were (as in the tragic instance of *Puritan*) or farther back. Consequently, the wise skipper-navigator checked his position, if he was quite unsure, with his sextant when he could get a shot. And the successful one, when he was about where he wanted to be, pinpointed himself with his lead, which he armed in the hollow in its bottom with a wad of butter, grease, or tallow.

Feeding the line over the rail, the skipper pulled it taut when he felt the lead plunk on the bottom, glanced at the fathom marker, and hauled it back aboard hand over hand, dripping. With a single heave he had both measured the depth of water against the charted depth and sampled the bottom, whether mud, sand, gravel, broken shells, or whatever. This obscure fragment of evidence could sometimes tell the knowing fisherman where he was in all that ocean—within a few hundred yards, if he had sounded and sampled there before—and, even more to the point, where the fish were liable to be.

This was the way of Leo Hynes, learned from the old-timers he had fished with, and once on the grounds he was back and forth between pilothouse and rail, sounding, sounding, ceaselessly feeling his way along the bottom forty, fifty, sixty fathoms and more below.

Summers, depending on the hour of arrival, the crew rolled out around four in the morning to slice bait into two-inch squares, more than twenty thousand of them, on the cutting boards that ran the length of the main cabintop on either side. *Adventure* might still be underway or just jogging under sail if Leo had sounded out

---

* For generations the Boston Lightship signaled the approach to Boston Harbor before it was replaced by an automated floating platform with a radiobeacon and horn. Marked on the chart as the Boston Diaphone, it is familiarly known to fishermen as the Bug Light.

Up from the bottom, now up again. JOHN CLAYTON PHOTO

his spot. The cutting took about an hour; baiting the hooks and carefully coiling the trawl back in the tub, another hour.

The two men in each dory normally fished three tubs of trawl. Each tub contained ten coiled fifty-fathom lines tied end to end, fifty-five hooks to a line, totaling 500 fathoms or 3,000 feet of trawl a tub, and 550 hooks, times three, end to end, for 9,000 feet of trawl, nearly 1¾ miles of line and 1,650 baited hooks a dory. Every hook was tied to the end of a lighter line about three feet long, a ganging (*gan-jin*), knotted every 5½ feet of so to the heavier trawl, or ground line, to minimize tangling.* Twelve dories, 20½ miles of trawl, 19,800 hooks to every set.

If the sea was not too choppy and the wind fair, Leo would set flying—steam

---

* To keep a ganging from slipping along the ground line when it was knotted, *Adventure*'s men dipped the end in kerosene, lighted it to burn the tar out, banged the flame out, and frayed the singed strands before tying. *Adventure* never advanced from the old cotton twine, which wore and rotted out in spite of its tarring, to the almost indestructible newfangled nylon.

Fred Thomas holds the stern alongside with his gaff. JOHN CLAYTON PHOTO

along at eight or nine knots and signal his men with a wave of his right or left arm to swing a dory out alternately to starboard or port and cast off when ready. Some of the more skittish complained it was like jumping off a racing freight train. In good weather he might drop them off over the course of two or three miles, closer if it was thick or nighttime.

When dropping his dories across the wind, Leo would set flying to leeward and slow down or drift almost to a stop before lowering to windward. If it was too bumpy or blowy to set flying, *Adventure* would lie-to or jog and send them off as from the hub of a wheel or in a semicircle. In the all-sail days, the schooners more commonly sent their dories forth in this pattern or, in the case of the flying set, dropped them back and loosed them from astern. Because of the limitations on maneuverability under sail alone, the trawls were left out much longer and frequently were underrun by the dories several times before being hauled back if the fish were biting. The auxiliary engine turned the flying set into an everyday practice at the hands of a skillful skipper, and although it had its hazards, as we shall see, the technique gave the dorymen more of a respite from the oars and spread the trawls over a broader area.

Readying each dory to go over the side, its crew hooked the dory tackles from the schooner's main and fore crosstrees into the rope loops, or beckets, in bow and stern and proceeded to "build her up," setting the thwarts in place and heaving in oars, mast, sail, and other light gear. The fellers hauled away at the tackles. The dory rose out of the nest and was swung over to the rail, where the tubs of trawl were lifted in. A final shove, a bit of slack on the tackles, the dorymates clambered up and over and in, and then they were hanging outside the rail, the sea rushing along a few feet beneath them. A dory's outfit: mast, boom, and sail; two barrels of fresh water and half-gallon jugs; trawl roller; two buoys with pole and flag target; two twenty-five-pound trawl anchors; two bailing scoops; two pairs of nippers for handling ground line; three kid boards to pen off the fish; tin foghorn; boat painter; three thwarts (seats); three sets of wooden tholepins for oarlocks (wood won't sink when lost overboard); one steering pin for sailing; four trawl-heaving sticks; dory knife; grappling iron and window weight to hold it down; one hook set; kerosene torch for night work; four ash oars; fish fork.*

On signal from Leo, they would lower away, and down she would drop with a spank and a splash, followed by one of the buoys. The stern fall was unhooked and cast off by the stern man. The cook or whoever was handy hung onto the painter while the bow fall was released, and when all was clear, let go and they were on their own. Bow man took to the oars while his mate astern threw over the first

---

* The cost of a locally made dory, fifteen feet on the bottom, was about $125, up to $140 (but still only $25 in Shelburne, Nova Scotia), in 1950 when John Clayton made this inventory. A complete outfit then, including dory, cost $500. Each tub of trawl was another $37.50, plus five dollars a thousand for hooks. A dory, under sentence of such hard labor, was only good for about three years.

anchor and commenced flicking the trawl out of the first tub with his short heaving stick so as not to get hooked himself. A good man could heave as fast as his mate could row. If the tide was slow, Leo would call to them while they were within earshot to "Tighten it up!"—throw the trawl more slowly so it would stay taut and not snarl on the bottom.

When the first tub was all out, the ground line was bent to the next, and then to the third, which was anchored and buoyed. The men might rest in their dories for as few as twenty minutes, time only for a smoke or two, before their taskmaster on *Adventure* guessed that the fish were biting and leaned on the air whistle that commanded them back to the task. Or it might be several hours, long enough to get picked up by the schooner for a mug-up, some dinner, or a quick flake (fisherman's parlance for a snooze).

Now for the backbreaker. Because it took about an hour per tub to haul the trawl, Hynes set his dories at least three hours before slack tide so that they wouldn't overrun and foul their trawls, which would be hauled before the current turned in the opposite direction and snagged them on something or other. This meant the

Captain Hynes hefts a pretty good halibut over the rail. JOHN CLAYTON PHOTO

The Compleat Angler 73

Top: *Another dory comes aboard as the quartet hauls in unison on the tackles.* JOHN CLAYTON PHOTO
Bottom: *From the splitting table, the cleaned fish are sloshed through the wash tub, then forked down the hatch for icing.* JOHN CLAYTON PHOTO

Top: *Up to their knees in their work, the gang labors to keep pace with Leo's luck.* JOHN CLAYTON PHOTO
Bottom: *Do we love fishin'? Wal, most o' the time.*
JOHN CLAYTON PHOTO

The Compleat Angler   75

boys were setting *with* the current, with nothing but bait on their hooks, but hauling every pound of fish from the bottom, and the entire burgeoning weight of the dory, against the current.

Bow man braced himself and swayed back on the ground line over the trawl roller, stuck in a hole in the forward gunwale, with every ounce of his strength, hand over hand, palms protected after a fashion by a pair of heavy rubber rings

Back at the Boston Fish Pier, Adventure *takes out. Plenty of basketfuls are required to move 80,000 pounds of fish up to the scales. Tied up astern is the steel beam trawler* Plymouth, *which came to the schooner's rescue and gave her a lee that black night in April of 1948 when she almost sank. They were in luck this trip. Sometimes the vessels would be four abreast at the Pier, and* Adventure*'s men would have to swing their catch across by way of a tackle from the intervening craft's jump stay.* JOHN CLAYTON PHOTO

One filling, one dumping, Jake Flores and Leo Romaine, with cigarette, play a duet on the winch alongside the Boston Fish Pier. JOHN CLAYTON PHOTO

called nippers.* It required the strength of both men when the bow was diving into a sharp chop or bouncing against a high ground swell and a four-knot current. Stern man grabbed the gangings as they marched aboard, hauled in the big, writhing fish, and slatted them off into the bottom of the dory, where a sort of hold, or kid, had been penned off by kid boards. He rebaited the bare hooks from the bait bucket and re-coiled the trawl back into its tub, ready for the next set.

(Anyone who has ever tried rowing an unloaded dory in a crosswind knows how hard it is to hold a course in such a high-sided, flat-bottomed craft and can imagine the plight of a couple of dorymen with a thousand pounds or more of fish in sharp seas and half a gale. "I was never scared in a dory, and I never went astray, not for very long anyway," claimed Mike O'Hearn, one of *Adventure*'s crew under Leo Hynes. "I thought I could always keep her on her bottom unless the wind lifted

* Faced with even more formidable fish to haul, the halibuters gained more purchase by replacing the trawl roller with a hurdy-gurdy, a primitive, hand-cranked winch clamped from gunwale to gunwale.

her right out of the water. I could always bring her bow to, but if it was too big a sea it was not good to bring her too sharp; just cant her to it a little.")

When the trawl snagged on the bottom, as was often unavoidable, they made it fast to the roller, took to the oars, and rowed ahead in an effort to free it. If it broke, or if a shark or dogfish had chewed it off—an added irritation when they were numerous in August—the cursing dorymates raised an oar, and Leo, who had been jogging around among his dories like an anxious sheepdog, would ease alongside in *Adventure* and tow them to their other buoy, to haul in the opposite direction. If it parted again, they anchored a buoy to mark the spot, broke out the grapple, and rowed across the line, hoping to hook it and salvage what they could.

A thousand pounds of fish would come up to the thwarts, half capacity but plenty to contend with in a sloppy sea. Up went the oar and Leo worked *Adventure* alongside, a tricky business. The engineer or the cook was thrown the painter. Up

Ease her off! And into the box with another basketful. Each box holds five hundred pounds of fish. With these baskets Adventure's *crew bailed her home in April 1948. JOHN CLAYTON PHOTO*

to their knees in them, the men pitched the fish with their forks up over the rail, and down when the waves decreed, and rowed back to resume the hauling. If near the end of the set and the sea wasn't too lumpy, they might say what the hell, and fill her up, bow and stern, to the dory's whole ton of capacity, or near it.

Picking up the dories gave all hands some nervous moments, most of all the man at the wheel:

"One of my worst enemies in the summertime was the fog. *Adventure* is pretty high in the bow, and the pilothouse was in the stern, and I had to be careful not to run somebody down. It was a big worry. The cook would be busy cooking, and the engineer in the engine room because she was controlled from there. I'd give Fred a bell to stop, and he'd start for the deck to grab the painter of the dory. We'd have too much way on, and I'd want to go astern. By the time he got back in the engine room, the dory was alongside, and the cook would be holding the painter, and she'd flip over because we had too much momentum.

"That happened several times. I flipped the dory and lost all the fish, and the men had to jump for the rail. It would have been a lot better if we'd had the pilot house up on top of the cabin house, with the engine controls up there. Don't know why we never did it."

One reason they didn't make a change was probably Fred's indubitable resistance to the remotest hint of remote control over his kingdom. Relocation of the steering wheel would have required a linkage of chains and pulleys back to the rudderstock. The unsatisfactory location of the pilothouse proved tragic. While Captain Hynes was taking a short leave to try the helm of the beam trawler *Boston College* in 1938 (he didn't like it), *Adventure* on August 22, under Captain Frank Mitchell, ran down one of her dories off Shelburne and capsized it. Ray Hubbard was rescued from the water; Theodore Babine drowned.*

As the dories came in, took out their fish, were "broken down" (gear hove out and thwarts set back flat on the bottom), and joined the rising nests, the men joined the rising force on deck. Some culled the fish by species and forked them into the kids that had been set up amidships; some split and gutted; others washed the dressed fish in the wash box of sea water aft on the port quarter before tossing them below to the gang that piled and iced the catch in the pens of the fish hold. In summer, the livers were flipped into steel drums, eighteen of them lashed to the forward bulwarks; they brought twenty-five dollars a drum for rendering into the vitamin-packed cod or haddock liver oil so distasteful to the growing children of the era.

And when the last fish was culled and cleaned and iced below, the last trace of gurry sent back to the sea, the bloody, slippery deck hosed down, the dinner

---

* Hynes also wondered why he never built a "whaleback," a sort of streamlined shelter ahead of the foremast in which the men could bait up and get lee from the wind and breaking seas. Beam trawlers had them, dory trawlers never did.

From dory to deck to hold to basket to box to cart, Adventure's *catch is about halfway to the dinner table.* JOHN CLAYTON PHOTO

bolted, and the coffee gulped, it was time for the second set—if the skipper was on the mark and the fishing the finest kind—and the entire exhausting procedure all over again.

Second set out and hauled and cleaned up by midnight with luck, you collapsed into your bunk all standing, with all but your oilskins and your boots on, and collapsed out again four hours later at four in the morning to begin your second twenty-four hour day highlining for In-and-Out Hynes.

On Georges Bank in the winter—that fierce and wicked riptide-ridden, storm-bedeviled shoal that has been the death of Gloucester for a century and a half—the men of the *Adventure* dared set no more than one tub at a time, drifting with the current, with a weight at the far end of the trawl. When conditions favored, Hynes would start them as early as one in the morning, in the pitch dark with only their flickering, smoking, stenching kerosene torches for light and a beggar's warmth, and *Adventure*'s deck lights to guide them home. That night and all through the next day, they would scout around in short sets, back and forth to the schooner, until they struck a school of codfish, and then they would work it for all it was worth.

Georges Bank a hundred years ago was the bane of the New England all-sail fisheries. Its cornucopian potential was discovered in the 1830s by handlining Gloucestermen, who at first were afraid to anchor and fish lest the fierce tidal currents pull their bows under. Storms took a terrible toll over the next fifty years, culminating on February 20, 1879, when a blizzard approaching hurricane strength devastated the winter fleet, sinking thirteen anchored Gloucester schooners with 143 men aboard—the worst disaster in the disastrous annals of the fisheries. Traditionally, the men dared not go dory trawling on Georges, nor would their skippers send them. Handlining from the rail was the rule. The more to be remarked that the men of *Adventure* rowed forth in their dories on this vast wilderness of water, fraught with such danger for vessels large and small, so courageously and so successfully.

It was Georges, the bastardly and the bountiful, that one day in January 1943 produced the biggest day that *Adventure* or Leo Hynes or any of his men ever had in all their lives.

"We had left Boston the day before, got on Georges about midnight and started fishing around one. My God, the codfish were numerous! We took the dories out all day long. The cook, the engineer and myself would jump down and fork the fish up ourselves for the fellers to get below for a bite to eat. We didn't even stop to clean. They stayed OK in the cold on deck. We started for home that evening, and the fish were rail to rail from one end to the other, right up to around the windlass. All twenty-four men started dressing them down. Good thing it was calm, or we could have lost the deckload.

"In twenty hours we caught 128,000 pounds of fish, and that must be some kind of a record for a dory trawler."

These twenty-two color photographs of Adventure *in her fishing days were taken by John Clayton with a 35mm camera during several of his seven trips aboard her between June 13, 1949, and November 3, 1953, when she was laid up. Selected from his large collection of Kodachrome slides, they are both the most representative and the best-preserved. A few others of documentary value but of lesser quality are printed in black and white elsewhere throughout the text. These pages comprise the only known photographic record in color of American dory trawling. Together with Clayton's 4-by-5-inch black and white photographs, they represent an unmatched archive of the last years of a way of life forever gone.*

With riding sail and jib triced up, Adventure *idles away from the Boston Fish Pier. The black of her topsides, in sombre contrast to her yellow name and stripe and the clean red of her hawse pipe (Captain Hynes rarely anchored, and never through the port bow), cannot hide her perky sheer. The red beam trawler at the wharf over her bow is the* **Plymouth,** *aft of which is the* **Lynn.** *The schooner beyond* Adventure*'s stern is probably the* **Marjorie Parker.**

Top: *The gang gathers by the starboard main shrouds, tying on
gangings from the bunches slung over their shoulders as they
make up a new trawl. Behind them, a dory hangs at the rail.
The black and yellow "Cape Ann hats" are of oiled or plasticized
cloth like their oilskins, similar to the old-fashioned
sou'wester except for the narrow, light-weather brim. From
the look of their beards, they have been at sea for a while.*
Bottom: *Sunburned hands tie a shiny new hook
to the business end of a ganging.*

Top: *Every one of a thousand hooks must be just so. A bent hook may not hold the bait — or the fish. The wooden hook-set, clamped on the rim of the trawl tub like a clothespin, holds a jig around which the hook is restored to its proper shape.*
Bottom: *Sharpening dull hooks. Note detail of the hook-set on the tub at left. On the cabin top beyond the coil of trawl are a dory torch and a collapsible canvas bucket.*

Left: *Readying for a night set,*
"Big Mac" MacDonald tops off
a dory torch with kerosene.
Below: *All hands pitch in at the*
bait board, set up to protect the
cabin top, slicing frozen herring.
"You cut it too big!" Leo would
fume at one notoriously slow baiter.
"We'll run out after three sets!"
Right: *A weathered old-timer baits*
up in the setting (or rising) sun.

Above: Dorymates "build up" the top dories
in both nests, setting thwarts in place, then
oars and trawl anchors hooked over the gunwale.
Either Adventure is fishing short, or two of
her usual twelve dories are already overboard.
Right: Port dory is up and over, hanging from
bow and stern tackles. In go the trawl tubs.
Oars, mast and sail, keg buoy with flag, and
anchors are aboard, thole pins at the ready
in the gunwales for the long pull.
Opposite page, top: "In with you, boys!"
Their mates stand at the shrouds with the
tackles, ready to lower away. The next
dories are already being built up.
Bottom, left: The stern man in a starboard
dory grabs for the hook to cast off the tackle.
Bottom, right: "Slow down, Leo!" On port side,
the stern man has thrown over the trawl buoy
and is going for the tackle. The bow man appears
to have unhooked the forward tackle, and the
dory is still being towed by the schooner.

<u>**Top:**</u> *Stout ash bends to stout heart, and they are off for the first set on a lonely sea.*
<u>**Bottom:**</u> *Up comes the trawl with a fish on. The dorymate coils it back in the tub. A trawl roller is in place in the bow at left but is not in use. The three-pronged fish fork is at the ready, and the extra-long bamboo buoy flagpole thrusts jauntily out of the stern.*

*On such a foggy day, the sun dancing through
the thick, Winslow Homer caught his Gloucestermen of a
hundred years ago, plying their trawls exactly so.*

*The men in number 5 must have parted their trawl, and
Adventure is giving them her version of a Nantucket sleigh
ride to the buoy at the other end of the line.*

*A fair wind on their tails, two of
Adventure's dories with a trip of fish sail
home to mother and the ever-knowing gulls.*

<u>Top</u>: *Splitting and gutting are not for the squeamish.*
A mess of fine haddock will soon be down the hatch
and iced while the skipper pushes on for the next set.
<u>Bottom</u>: *Back at the Boston Fish Pier, a study*
in trawl tubs and hard fishing.

<u>Top</u>: *Seaworn, workworn, and manworn, and bereft of all her fishing
gear but her dories, the Old Lady steams up Boston Harbor on her
last trip of her first career, November 3, 1953. The Charlestown
Navy Yard is dead ahead, the new Mystic River Bridge beyond her
mainmast, and just before it, hard astarboard, Chelsea Creek.*
<u>Bottom</u>: *Done fishing, Adventure awaits her fate at Munroe's
wharf in Chelsea Creek. The prospects look none too good.*

Whacking across Penobscot Bay at 13½ knots, a rejuvenated Old Lady leaves you breathless. CAPTAIN DOUG LEE PHOTO.

Born-again **Adventure**'s *main cabin, restored and resplendently furnished, remains essentially the same under Captain Sharp as it was in the days of captains Thomas and Hynes. Looking forward through the former engine room, now partially occupied by "Cabin Small" and the piano (the intervening bulkhead has been removed) along the passage dividing the old fish hold.* NEAL PARENT PHOTO.

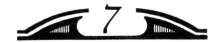

Spots

When I was a young man I used to be up all night sounding around, trying to find a place to get fish. One time Captain Parsons in the Lark *complimented me by saying, "You'll get fish, Leo. I know you're up all night sounding around." That made me feel good, because Parsons was a professional. He'd been around a long time.*

Leo Hynes

zaak Walton immortalized the art of casting into the meadowed streams of England, but he was not thinking of the commercial fishermen when he rejoiced that "angling will prove to be so pleasant that it will prove to be, like virtue, a reward to itself." A fish a man or less, pleasant as that sounds on a dreamy summer afternoon, was no great reward aboard the good schooner *Adventure*.

One hundred and twenty-eight thousand pounds in twenty hours, however, was sufficient reward to itself. So was a record stock in 1943 of $364,000, which put food in bellies, shirts on backs, coal in cellars, and even a few gallons of war-rationed gasoline in the tank. Reward enough, considering the virtues of dory trawling, man to fish.

We have looked into the technique of it in some detail. What of the art? How, in all that vast Atlantic, did old In-and-Out Hynes discover the unseen prey?

One word: sounding. Up all night sounding around, as Parsons the professional admired. Part of him in the pilothouse, poring over his charts and his notes, ducking out to heave his lead up and down a thousand miles of ocean, marking the depths against the chart, feeling and tasting the stuff that came up on the butter, checking his taffrail log. And part of him sixty fathoms down in the murk, swimming along the bottom, responding to the shifting tides, nosing around for dinner.*

Summers, generally, Hynes took *Adventure* down beyond Cape Cod to the South Channel, the deep between Georges Bank, the Cape, and Nantucket Shoals, except when the dogfish hit in the late springtime, and then they might have to cruise as far east as Sable Island Bank and even farther, to the colder waters of Banquereau—"Quero"—heading toward the Grand Bank.

The dogfish are the minions of the devil, small sharks of three feet or so that sweep through the seas like plagues of underwater locusts, attacking everything within sight and smell. Baited hooks are their meat. The sight and smell of the thrashing, line-tangling, useless "dogs" writhing up over the side of the dory on ganging after ganging was enough to turn the toughest stomach after a while. When the cooler weather and water came around with fall, *Adventure* headed for the nearer banks, Cashes Ledge closer in to the eastward, and those rimming the Gulf of Maine: Georges, Browns, and La Have.

It was all up to the skipper where and when they fished and how often; it was up to his experience, his strength, his drive, his intuition, his fish sense. The year-in and year-out highliners like In-and-Out Hynes swore they could smell them. The Great South Channel was Leo's happy—most of the time—hunting ground.

"I'd never be eating with the gang but busy sounding around. Had a good fishing hole down there, eight or ten miles long. It took hours to find it sometimes. A bed of mussels. Sound on that, and you'd know because the shells would make a sharp cut on the butter. Just south of that was a spot of sand; no fish there. Mud with grit in it, the fish would be feeding there, but never on sand or slime. Sometimes I'd anchor my spot buoy over that mussel ground. It was just a bamboo pole eighteen or twenty feet long, with a flashlight bulb and batteries strapped on, and weighted. The draggers would see us setting out there and catching fish, and they'd try it and get hung right up on that rough bottom."

When he first went skipper, Leo was fooled plenty by the old-timers, especially Ernest Parsons, who would come upon *Adventure*'s spot buoy with its tiny twinkling light awaiting the dawn, and cover the ground with his own dories. Parsons hailed from New Harbor, Newfoundland, and was cut out of the same cloth as Hynes. The fleet called his schooner *Lark* the "Channel Express," so fast and so full did he bang back and forth between the South Channel and the Fish Pier. Another trickster was Fred Wilson in the schooner *Shamrock*. Hynes had to get up earlier than Wilson, too.

---

* It was where the chart left off that the art began. For instance, just before Leo Hynes took over *Adventure*, Albert Close of London published the formidably detailed *Fishermen's and Yachtsmen's Chart, Cape Cod to Newfoundland. Fishing Banks Information from the Fisheries Depts. of the U.S., Canadian and French Govts. Rough Ground Marked by Gloucester, Nova Scotia and Newfoundland Skippers.* Primarily intended for the skippers of beam trawlers loath to rip their nets to shreds, the chart indicates the type of bottom around the banks, areas suited for dragging, tide rips, and some fish habitats.

"One evening we hadn't found much in the Channel, and I was about to steam for Georges, a hundred miles up. The *Shamrock* was there. So I went up. I knew Fred well. He'd been crew with me. And I says, 'Did you find any fish today?' 'Not a damn thing,' says he. We hadn't gone very far when I saw him drop a dory over. I turned right around and came back, and I says, 'You musta told me a damn lie. Why're you putting a dory over if you haven't found any fish?' He says, 'Don't mind me, I'm crazy.' So we stayed right there and next day got plenty of fish.

"But sometimes he'd come up and say, 'How's the fishing, Leo?' I'd say, 'Oh, I haven't got a thing.' He'd say, 'You're loaded awful deep not to have any fish.' I guess he guessed how I was doing."

A doryman's chores are never done. Between trips (precious little layover fishing with In-and-Out Hynes) there is trawl to check out and repair— and dory sails needing attention. The fish liver barrels are lashed to the rails in the bow. Though twenty-five years old, the windlass is like new; Adventure's skippers had little use for anchors. JOHN CLAYTON PHOTO

You had to watch those guys every minute. To foil Parsons and Wilson and the others who had learned to follow him like a hunter behind a pointer, In-and-Out would find his spot, then steam a few miles away and drop his buoy. After they had raced in and set all their dories on what they hoped were his fish, *Adventure* would run back over her course and glean her rightful reward.

"I found this little spot of shallow water just nor'west of the Cultivator buoy on the edge of Georges and sounded gravel bottom. My God, the fish were all over it! We got 50,000, mostly haddock, in one day, and when we came in, it was unbelievable to the other fishermen. I couldn't find it all the time, but when I located it permanently they'd all follow me, especially Parsons. Such a small spot, it would fish out quickly, so I'd head down there only every few weeks.

"Parsons would follow me. I'd put out my stern light to lose him, locate the spot, steam ten miles away, and when dawn came pretend I was sounding, and he'd do the same. Course he wouldn't get any kind of a bottom to fish, and it would be getting late, so he'd steam north where he was sure they were, and when he was out of sight we'd slip over to our spot there on the edge of the bank where the cliff comes up to the Continental Shelf. You could get between sixty and forty fathom, and all kinds of fish, and the draggers couldn't get in there to disturb them. We'd fill up and be home long before the rest. I pulled that stunt many times."*

Some spots were too small.

"When the fathometer came in (I think we were the first of the dory fishermen to have one, around 1938), we were bound out one day, and I was playing around with it. About sixty miles from the Lightship and thirty short of the grounds I ran across this little spot, just a nubble of shallow water. I circled around it, and in the morning we could get only eight dories on it. They got 50,000 pounds and made our week's pay. The other four dories were in deeper water and got nothing. We went right back to market. But it was so damn small I could never find it again."

Some spots were too deep.

"We set in the deep water between the northern end of Georges and Browns one day. My God, the cusk were numerous! Filled her up, 100,000 of cusk and 50,000 of cod. Weren't sure just where we were, I think about 185 miles from the Lightship, but we were lucky to get the trawls back. There was so much tide there, and deep water, 130 fathoms or so. Though tempted, I never set there again. Too dangerous. We might have lost everything. Awful for the men, hauling in all that tide, but not a complaint."

Some spots were deceptive.

* Of the famous rivalry between the schooners *Lark* and *Adventure*, and Captains Parsons and Hynes, the latter reflected in *his* later years: "Parsons was much older than I was and always top dog. And then I started to beat him a little, and he'd get mad as hell. He had a cottage near us in New Hampshire. We didn't socialize much together, but one time we were having some drinks, and his second wife, who was about thirty years younger than he was, told him, 'Parsons, you might as well admit that age has got to give way to youth.' And he says, 'Wal, I s'pose so.'"

Trawls get a final going-over. They're under way for one of the skipper's "spots." Smooth seas, not much wind, engine throbbing, dory sail drying. The air horn with which Leo summons his dories faces forward atop the exhaust stack at right. JOHN CLAYTON PHOTO

"We were off the no'theast bar of Sable Island, which extends about twelve miles out. You could see the breakers. I dropped the dories off right along and said, 'Now row towards the bar.' The crew was scared to death. They wouldn't row at all. They threw out all the trawl and told me, 'Gee, we're gonna be in the breakers!' Now we were two miles away, and I knew the fish was right up against the breakers. And I knew the trawls wasn't gonna reach that far. We had more snarls that day, them throwing them over like that and not rowing in, and I bawled the hell outta them: 'For Chrissake, don'tcha trust me?'"*

* Captain Hynes took the *Gertrude L. Thebaud* into about the same spot before he had *Adventure* and caught 7,000 pounds of halibut. "We could hear the breakers all the time. It was thick o' fog, breakers right behind us, but we got used to it. I slept on the floor in my oilskins, and the crew kept coming down and waking me up, saying that we were getting too close. The currents are real bad around Sable."

*Captain Hynes places a call on the first ship-to-shore radio-telephone
installed in a dory trawler. "You put it in," the dealer told Leo, "and I'll
give you a radio-phonograph for your home." It was a deal.* JOHN CLAYTON PHOTO

Some spots proved elusive.

"I used to try a lotta places what the old-timers never fished before, and it
would pay off. There was one 110 miles east-southeast from Boston, nowhere near
Georges, and a lot of haddock. This evening we left Boston, and I said that we'll set
everything and whatever we get we're going home with. I anticipated 50,000 pounds.
We set, and hardly a fish. I sounded, and nothing but slimy old mud. I went back
and looked at the log, and instead of 110 miles, it was a hundred. I'd misread it.
The day was wasted. All that work, and I bet we didn't get a thousand pounds. I
felt like committing suicide."

Some spots were pinpoints.

"We found a good haddock spot on Browns. It was protected by an old wreck,
because some of the hooks came up covered with rust and old paint."

Some spots were nonexistent.

"The fellers didn't like to sound at night, 'specially in the cold and the wind,

*To help find those spots out there in the middle of watery nowhere, her owners gave **Adventure** an early Loran in the main cabin. And she was probably the first dory trawler to carry a depth sounder, as early as 1939. She never had radar. For most of her days fishing, it was compass, sextant, sounding lead, and the **Old Man's** ability to think like a fish.* JOHN CLAYTON PHOTO

and one time one of 'em dropped the lead in the ash bucket and brought it down to me. Course I knew it was ashes right off when I saw it and said to him, 'Looks like we're down to Maggie Wallace's.'" (Maggie was the proprietress of the Wayside Inn, a renowned barroom on the Gloucester waterfront.)

Some spots were shrouded in the fog and black of night.

"Down where we fished on the South Channel in the summertime there was a bank of fog south from the Pollock Rip Lightship off Chatham on the elbow of the Cape that would hardly ever clear up, while north of it there wouldn't be any at all. I'd tell the boys that if they got lost in that fog they should sail north on the prevailing sou'west wind toward the Cape, and I'd steam north in *Adventure* til I got out of the fog bank, and put on all the lights. Sure enough, every time, they got back on board during the night, time enough for us to get back on the spot in the morning."

And Henry Abbott remembers it well.

"We was down on the South Channel, in the dories, an' 'bout four in the afternoon the fog shut in. So we sailed north. Well, 'bout one in the mornin' we suddenly saw the light flashin' on *Adventure*, an' there was Leo. He'd sailed all night toward shore, figurin' which way we'd go. The fog cleared an' he found us. He said, 'You fellers better turn in. Yer all cold an' wet.' We said, 'Naw, we're OK.' An' we started baitin' up fer the next set. We were all out in the dories agin between two an' three."

Some spots were shrouded in forgetfulness.

"We were just about to leave for a trip, had to catch the tide, when Phil Manta came running down and said to call Lil. Feller I went to school with, was in the Canadian Air Force, and a buddy, wanted to make a trip.* It was September, I think just before the war. I said, 'Send 'em down. I'll wait.' Soon as we got out the wind came no'theast. There was no room below, so they said they'd spread their sleeping bags way up forward on each side of the windlass. Well, old *Adventure* took a dive in the night, and they washed back clear to the dories, their bags full o' water. I had to sleep 'em behind the steps in the main cabin.

"We couldn't find any fish to the west'ard and went on to try La Have Bank. Couple of the young fellers, Tom Fowler and George Grant, forgot to take their torch with them in the dory. Dark comes early there in the fall. All the others came back aboard, and they were missing. No sense steaming around. Probably never find 'em, or run 'em down. We had all the deck lights on. It started to breeze up. Finally they came aboard after two or three hours. They'd parted their trawl and rowed up to the other buoy, and then had to row like hell, because I was a distance off. I blasted 'em!"

And Tom Fowler remembers that night well, too.

---

* The buddy was Roy Stanley (Bill) Grandy, a native of Bay l'Argent, six years older than Leo Hynes. Grandy was a pioneer Canadian pilot and RCAF flyer who served in both world wars. He died in 1965 at the age of seventy-one.

"Me and 'Maggie' Grant were sure lost all right and never thought we'd make it. We hugged Leo when we got aboard!"

And some spots just disappeared.

"It was New Year's Day. We had 30,000 of fish aboard, and I was feeling good, and I told the fellers we'd make this one more set and go home. The wind was just coming up from the east. We were on the edge of Browns, two in the morning. I sounded in fifty fathoms, knew right where we were, and steamed off and set the dories no'theast and sou'west with thirty tubs of trawl. I knew it was gonna breeze up, but I underestimated the tide, and coming back—we'd been set down by it so far to the nor'west—I sounded ninety fathom.*

"Well, I says to myself, the hell with it, we'll trust to luck. They set and laid on 'em for half an hour, and I flashed the lights and blew the whistle to haul back. My God, what a mess, the tide setting us into that deep water! Before daylight I had 'em all back aboard. One saved half a trawl. Some lost their anchors; the lines parted off. No one came back with whole gear, and no fish besides. Went back for the buoys at daylight, and they were all gone. The tide had taken them under. Nothing left. Thirty tubs gone, at fifteen dollars a tub.

"So we went into Shelburne to refit, and in come a blinding snowstorm. There was an old friend of mine, a Nova Scotian, who got in just ahead of us. He said, 'Leo, don't worry about it. Let's go up to the dance and have a couple drinks, and I'll get you your gear tomorrow for wholesale price.' And he did, half the Boston cost. We went out and had a pretty good trip. He didn't have a radio on his vessel, and I bought him the best I could find and gave it to him next time I saw him. He was pretty pleased."

Although *Adventure* was a line trawler for the common deepwater species first and last, she did not turn up her knockabout nose in the midsummer months for a chance at the king of the pelagic jungle, the swordfish.

No wily Waltonian arts here. No stalking of the shadowy depths with a buttered lead. Blind luck, mostly, and a good aim and a strong arm. The sleek speedster with the pointy upper jaw, weighing up to several hundred pounds, cruised in from the open ocean in July and August to compete with the fishermen on the offshore banks. With a bellyful of mackerel, haddock, squid, or whatever chanced in the way of its slashing proboscis, yon swordfish enjoyed lazing on the surface of the summer sea, betrayed only by the tips of its dorsal fin and tail.

A few of the regular skippers with the bent and the yen were in the habit of taking time off from dory trawling to go swordfishing for the summer, as others did for the mackerel seining.

* Of Browns Bank, the Albert Close *Fishermen's and Yachtsmen's Chart* cautions: "Fishermen report it foul on the western shoal, rough with coarse sand, gravel, pebbles and rocks over the remainder and black stones on its eastern end in 45 fathoms. Fishermen work in 20 to 75 fathoms. Fish:. Cod, Halibut, Haddock, and some Pollock and Hake. Fishermen and other authorities report that the Tidal Streams on Browns Bank occasionally run to the N.E. continually for 15 hours at 2 knots. Tide diagrams near this bank should be used with caution after strong winds."

Leo Hynes was of the pragmatic class who recognized a dividend that was no more than a diversion when he saw it, so he kept his dories fishing, carried a few harpoons, and tacked on a summer pulpit about seven feet long. He had it hinged outboard of *Adventure*'s bowspritless bow so that it could be lifted out of the way with the jib halyard when they were nosing into the wharf.

Now and again they came across a swordfish and preached eternity to it with the iron of their harpoon, but never again like the day, just before sundown, when *Adventure* was heading home with a trip. On the edge of Georges, she ran into a veritable school of them, "finning," hundreds of them. Leo was almost beside himself with excitement, and so was his crew.

"Wherever we looked there were swordfish. Half the men were aloft, the rest on deck, and they were all shouting, 'Go here! Go there!' My God, what chaos! One

Big Mac in the bow. Who else? Look at the stern out of the water.
Probably his patient dorymate at the oars is Henry Abbott. The buoy
and buoy line are over, marking the starting end of their trawl, and
they're off into the haze to try the skipper's spot. JOHN CLAYTON PHOTO

of the crew was pretty good at striking them, but we missed more than we hit. Thirteen swordfish we got that evening."

That was the collective swordfish adventure. The singular one starred Leo Hynes, the Intrepid Lone Harpooner, and a cast of doubtful support consisting of the Old Lady and her Engineer. Therefrom hangs a tale.

The dories were out tending the trawls this one fine day, leaving Captain Hynes aboard *Adventure* with Engineer Fred, and Pat Nolan down in the galley, cooking as always, when the Skipper spied the sharklike fin and telltale tail of the Big One up ahead, just basking, alone on the ocean. The Skipper grabbed a harpoon, ran to the rail, and with a mighty heave he ironed him. The Big One dove like a comet. The line was zinging out. But how to get it back—and him aboard?

The two dories left on deck were all dried out—they were spares and hardly ever in the water, not even rained on. They leaked like baskets, but the Skipper managed to get one of them swung up. Somehow he jackassed it over the rail and into the water and jumped in.

Now the Skipper should have known better. The bottoms of plenty of dories were pierced by enraged swordfish, their overeager occupants sometimes wounded, and on at least one occasion, killed. Those swords are up to five feet long and not for fencing.

A dried-out dory with the seams opened up to the daylight no doubt added to the zest of the chase. The Skipper might have paused to recall, before he lowered away that day, the spring when he first took *Adventure* and had her hauled for her annual fitting-out on the marine railway at Gloucester. In two weeks she was back over, and they went fishing.

"I dropped the dories off at night, over about two miles, when I heard the men shouting in the last one. We went over, and they were almost swamped. My God, they were bailing for their lives! We picked them up and went back, and all the rest were yelling and bailing too. Nobody ever thought of putting water in 'em while we were hauled, and they dried out. Had to go in under the lee of Cape Ann and run them out in a string the whole next day to swell up. Lost two days' fishing."

But the lesson of that day was lost in the excitement of this one, and the Skipper jumped in the leaky dory in his ardor to boat the Big One.

"Well, I got him up fast enough, but by God I didn't have anything to hold onto his tail out of the water to haul him up on deck, and he took off and went down again. What a job I had! I didn't care if I lost him or not by that time, but I finally got him up again.

"Swordfishermen have a gaff that they hook into the tail and flip them up with while they put a strap around it, but I didn't have anything like that. Finally I got him, and I was holding onto his tail with both hands. The damn leaky dory was half full of water by now, and me slipping and sliding around in it.

"I hollered up to the Engineer, 'Back up the vessel up there!' Well, old Fred wasn't the fastest guy in the world, and he had on low, slippery shoes, and so did I, because I hadn't stopped to put on my Red Jacks. He plodded down to the engine room and started backing the vessel. By the time he come back on deck to take a look, I could see he was backing too fast and yelled, 'Slow her down!' So he slid below again, but before he could, she backed right over me.

"The dory was pretty near awash, but it worked kind of logily out from under the quarter. We finally got a line on him and got him aboard. But never again for me. Never again would I fool with a swordfish when all the dories were out."

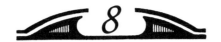

The Lionhearts

Since the introduction of trawl fishing, some twelve years since, another peril has been added to the fisheries, viz.: that of being lost from the dories while visiting trawls, or estrayed during the fog which oftentimes shuts in on the fishing grounds, enveloping them like a pall.

The Fishermen's Memorial and Record Book
Gloucester, 1873

he glass was down, and there was no doubt that something was afoot from the southeast. *Adventure* was cruising west of Sable Island along the bank, and Captain Leo Hynes, after some general consultation with his crew, decided to make one test set before it breezed up and then to run back to the westward under the coming southeasterly. It was the first of April, 1936. He was rounding out his second year with the still young Lady, who was rounding out her tenth.

So they put the dories over, and the men had not been working the trawls an hour when the wind was blowing forty knots. Skipper called them back. They rowed in against it, taking plenty of water over their bows, and were soon all around *Adventure*, on the windward side and in the lee, trying to hold off or hold in with their oars. Leo strove to head *Adventure* into the southeasterly while they worked tackles on both sides, hooking and lifting half-swamped dories that rose and fell while alternately whacking against her and diving away.

One of those dives got the better of a dory, and over it flipped, dumping its occupants, who succeeded in flailing back to their capsized craft and grabbing the plug strap on the bottom until lines could be flung to them from deck. That strap probably saved their lives. Without it, the flat bottom and flaring sides presented nothing to hang on to. Dories had always been fitted with a wooden plug jammed into a drain hole in the bottom. The guy who ran the first rope loop through the dory plug from the outside should have been given a medal.

The next dory to flip was occupied by Big John Santos, a Portuguese who had fished with *Adventure* for several years, and his mate. Mike O'Hearn and Archie Hubbard in their dory, and Henry Abbott and Titus Wamboldt, a lanky Lunenburger long with Leo, in theirs, tried to reach the two men in the water.* Big John's dorymate made it to the plug strap and was saved.

Abbott never forgot that moment: "Big John was a good swimmer, but he had on his boots an' all. Titus was a tall, strong Dutch feller. He kep' rowin' an' we thought we could git to Big John. We could see his head bobbin' up an' down. But jest as we got to him he sunk. He prob'bly got panicky. Should of stayed with his dory with the other man. That was a bad day. Big John Santos was a helluva nice shipmate."

At half-mast, Leo sailed home to the news that Lil had borne them their Patricia. One lost, one gained.

Winters. Those winter trips into the North Atlantic stuck in Hynes's head like pins in a battle map.

"The first day on Browns was fine, and we got 35,000 pounds. Then it blew an easterly gale for five days. I finally got 10,000 more and decided to go to Portland, as 45,000 was too small a trip to go all the way to Boston. Off Mount Desert Island it came nor'west, a veritable hurricane. I guess we waited too long to get that 10,000, because there was not enough easterly left to get us beyond Mount Desert on our way to Portland.

"*Adventure* was icing up. The seas were coming aboard and freezing, and we were chopping ice all the time. We gave up Portland and ran for Shelburne. Had no steam, like the beam trawlers, and had to chop by hand. What a job to get it off the dories! We rounded Brazil Buoy past Cape Sable, which put us beam to it, and I thought she'd roll over with the weight of that ice on deck.

"We had Dutch-type half-doors on the pilothouse, and the water was coming in and rolling over the vessel and the house, everything awash, trickling down the hatch into the cabin. We were really worried. The ice was so thick that you could just squeeze down a hole in the forward companionway."

Chopping ice was the way Captain Jeff went. The trip stuck with Henry Abbott, too.

"Began icin' up comin' in. Everybody was gittin' worried. You couldn't see

_____

* Mike O'Hearn later was a well-known skipper even better known as "Mike Dempsey" for his resemblance to the Manassa Mauler. Four decades later, the episode reminded him of another: "I set dories myself when the glass was 29. Not too many done that and got away with it. It was a fine day. I says, if it breezes up we'll put out a buoy and get the gear the next day. I didn't think the gang would go. But we got 40,000 of fish, and coming home, it struck—yeah, a sou'wester!"

nothin' fer the vapor. The sea was bad but not right high. Wherever it hit it made ice. Got so bad after three days we couldn't pound it off. She started to leak in the bulwarks. She was wobbly, heavy. We were scared if she took enough water, an' the engine conked out, we was in fer the grave.

"I come on deck fer my watch, an' Leo says, 'Keep her off, Henry.' That night she was goin' to one side an' the other, an' Leo says he hoped nothin' would happen to the engine. She was down so low, water was all over the deck. Dories was one solid cake of ice. Even the gangways, you had to slide to git down, forrard an' aft. Jest had the foresail up, all iced, couldn't git it down. One man, an oldish feller, was runnin' 'round moanin' how foolish he was to come out here, gonna get lost.

"You had to keep yer face muffled up with a rag. Seemed like yer skin was just burnin'. You could only stay on deck a few minutes an' then had to run down below. Like a burn in hot water.

"We went down an' down an' down into Shelburne. Got a towboat 'longside with steam, an' it took two or three days to git the ice off. We come near gittin' our mouth full o'water then, don't think we didn't."

Some gales blew cold, some blew hot, and some blew both.

They had been jogging one tack for seven straight days between the heel and toe of Browns—meaning the southeast and northeast edges of the bank, which is shaped like a lady's old-fashioned high-button shoe—and *Adventure* was icing up. Leo:

"One morning I hollered to the watch, 'What's the weather like up there?' 'It's foggy, skipper.' 'Foggy? Can't be, with the wind nor'west and still blowing.' But it was, and right thick.

"'Draw a bucket of water,' I said. And we felt the temperature. You could swim in it. We were blown seventy miles off the edge of the shelf into the Gulf Stream. That melted all the ice on the vessel, and just as quick as going to Shelburne. So I decided that the next time we got caught that far to the south'ard, we might as well send her off the southern end and melt the ice in the bargain, if there was any."

Sometimes it was blowing and snowing.

In the wintertime you had to sneak in a set when you could and take your chances. One particular day, the wind had moderated, and Leo had found a spot. He put the dories over for a one-tub test just before dark. They came back with fish, and he dropped the spot buoy. *Adventure* jogged while the boys chowed and baited up, and at midnight he sent them back out. The glass was dropping, and the wind had come up from the southeast, and it was just beginning to snow, but they agreed to try it. The tide was running northeast and southwest, so they had to throw their trawls against a crosswind.

"I stayed with a couple of the dories in the middle, watching the torches. The snow was thickening. The two parted their trawls, which left five dories on each side of the vessel, with a hole in the middle, so I flashed the deck lights for them to

Captain Hynes chews on his cigar and ponders the future—in the form of the modern dragger behind him. It is January 1952, and he is fifty-one and nearing the end of his dory-trawling days. JOHN CLAYTON PHOTO

come in. They didn't respond at once, and boy, I blasted 'em for it! With everything else going on, one of the men came aboard with a hook deep in his flesh, and I had to stop and cut it out.

"The last dory got on board at daylight. The wind was increasing so that we couldn't get the fish out of it. The men jumped for the rail for their lives, and we hoisted the dory, fish and all, on board. Stowed the tubs below and lashed the dories. By God, a sea came up and washed all the fish off the deck! Some night that was! At the worst of it, I thought I was gonna lose everyone."

And sometimes merely blowing. Henry Abbott again:

"One time Leo had the flag up in the riggin' to come in 'cause he seen there was a gale o' wind comin' up right savage, seas too rough, an' we were goin' to git it. My dorymate an' me was a good distance away an' was foolish enough to keep our fish. When we come down it was so rough we couldn't hardly git aboard. We pitched up our fish, an' the *Adventure* rolled so much I declare to God you could see her keel.

"We got aboard, an' Leo give the wheel to someone an' climbed up in the forrard riggin' to steer the vessel to the dories, "'cause it was pilin' up right quick, an' I went in the after riggin' to spot 'em. An' be Christ, Leo's oil hat blew off his head an' hit me fair in the kisser, right in me face. An' I says, 'Leo, I got yer hat all right!'"

As Henry and his skipper knew well enough, there are two occasions in life that you laugh: when it's funny, and when it isn't. The rest of the time, at sea anyway, you had just better keep your mouth shut—and pray if the occasion is appropriate.

So it was, toward the end of March 1940, out on *Adventure*'s familiar spot, the instep of Browns. Late afternoon, blowing a brisk thirty knots from the southwest and the glass dropping. One last set before dark, said the Old Man, and over with the dories. They were out there hauling when two of them parted their trawl and rowed out to their outer buoys to pick up the other ends.

That was when the barometer said I told you so, and the fog rolled in. The two were two miles from the rest of the dories, somewhere in the "enveloping pall." It didn't help matters when the breeze veered to the northwest and piped up. Leo blew his air whistle, but only ten dories came in. He jogged *Adventure* around for an hour, blasting on the whistle to no avail. Four of his men had been swallowed up. He headed north for Shelburne to report to the Canadian Coast Guard and spread the word, though the heavy hearts around him knew no dory could long survive a forty-knot gale.

Seven hours passed when *Adventure*'s old rival, Ernest Parsons, haddocking not far off in the *Lark*, heard the bleat of a dory horn carried eerily on the wind and picked up Leo's brother, Jeremiah Hynes, and Jerry's dorymate, Frank Mouzer, neither of them much the worse for it, and took them into Boston when he finished his trip.

Arriving at Shelburne in *Adventure*, Captain Hynes sounded the alarm and telephoned his childhood friend, Bill Grandy, the Canadian Air Force pilot who had washed back to the dories that windy night in his sleeping bag. The two were about to embark on an air search in a flying boat from Halifax when they got the word that the other two had been rescued by a British freighter in the Bay of Fundy. Trying for the coast, Maxwell Banfield and James Miles had raised sail in the fog but missed Cape Sable and passed clear up into Fundy. They had gone forty-two hours without food in the bitter cold and were delirious from exposure when the freighter chanced upon them.

And still game. Their rescuers landed Banfield and Miles at Halifax, where they grabbed the next train for Lunenburg, and then on to Shelburne, and back aboard *Adventure* to finish out their trip.

In the bad old days of sail out of Gloucester, such incidents of dorymen going astray and making it into land or being picked up after days of the most awful suffering at sea, or never making it, were so commonplace that their recitation merited a mere paragraph in the local paper.*

On a similar occasion *Adventure* was fishing on La Have Bank, seventy or eighty miles southeast of Cape Sable, when a soup of a fog rolled in just as Leo was towing a dory that had parted its trawl up to the buoy. Dark was coming on when he went back to pick up the others, and they had disappeared, totally, without a sound. All night he searched at the dire risk of running one down, jogging under sail, wind southwest, and not a sign or a sound of twelve dories—the whole twelve dories and twenty-four men. Their skipper was frantic.

But the next morning the rising sun burned through the fog, and there they were, off on the horizon, all headed for the coast in a flotilla. They had stuck together through the night, blowing their horns to keep contact, and on the chance that he'd hear them, put up their sails and struck off a compass course for land.

Fog at sea is rarely a subject of amusement among mariners, and even under the best of circumstances, fog stories have a damp twist to them.

Adventure was picking her way home to Boston through the fog one day, Leo puzzling over the chart, the lookout up forward trying to identify buoys.

"Thick? Why we went up to the west'ard looking for a buoy, couldn't see a thing it was so thick. Finally we saw a lobster boat and went up to him and asked, 'Where in hell are we?' And he said, 'Cap, don't go any farther or you'll be on the merry-go-round.' We were damn near into Revere Beach.**

"Another time, one April, we were up on Browns north of the toe, and it came no'theast, one of the worst gales I was ever in, and we drifted all the way down to Georges. Came into Boston, so thick o' fog we missed the buoy and couldn't find it. I'd called Lil on the radio to meet me. We didn't know where we were, and I was so tired I just turned old *Adventure* around and went back outside again til morning. Poor Lil waited all night long on the Fish Pier while I slept in my bunk."

The newspapers and the radio were full of foreboding—of der Führer's threatened coups and "protectorates" in Europe and of Neville Chamberlain's "Stop Hitler Movement"—when *Adventure* sailed from Boston for Georges on Saturday, the eleventh of March, 1939.

When they reached the grounds the next day, a storm was most certainly in

---

* Not so Howard Blackburn, who froze his hands around his oar handles and rowed over sixty miles into Newfoundland with the refrigerated corpse of his dorymate after they were separated from the *Grace L. Fears* on Burgeo Bank in a blizzard in 1883. It took Blackburn five days without food or water, and he lost all his fingers and several toes to gangrene, and almost his life. Years later, the greatest doryman of them all made two lone crossings of the Atlantic in small sloops, among other exploits, and ran a celebrated saloon where young Leo Hynes, fresh to Gloucester, in awe watched the great man palm dimes off the bar.

**Captain Hynes had a similar experience in the *Gertrude L. Thebaud* coming home from Sable Island Bank, pressing for the Boston market with only an old sextant and a compass for navigation, thick all the way. They couldn't even find the Boston Lightship. "We came across a boat hauling lobster pots, and by God we were in Scituate Harbor, inside the little breakwater!" Scituate is on the South Shore of Boston, and Leo had surely missed the Lightship by eight miles. The harbor is so small that he must have had to back out the *Thebaud* or go aground.

the offing. It was in the air, the look and the feel and the tension of what the fishermen call a weather breeder. That night, sure enough, it breezed up from the northeast. By Monday morning, the thirteenth, the front had struck, engulfing them in blasts of wind that sucked down from the heavens and swept up from the sea, alternating droves of rain, sleet, spindrift, and snow.

The schooner was in the Gully between Georges and Browns, near the northeast peak of Georges in perhaps 130 fathoms. The waves were by now alarmingly high, pitched up sharp and steep as they gained energy racing over the shoals before the gale and then met head-on the opposing tide coursing through the Gully.

By early afternoon most of the seas roaring and hissing down on them were judged to be thirty feet from trough to crest, and the wind screamed through the rigging as if to rip it away. All they were carrying was the main riding sail, and that was more than she wanted. The dories had long since been lashed down.

At about two in the afternoon Captain Hynes called all hands to take in the riding sail and heave the loose fishing gear on deck into the fishhold in case they were swept, which was more likely by the minute, for *Adventure* was pitching, plunging, lunging, rolling, and laboring, and having great difficulty holding her own. It looked then to be blowing close to seventy-five, Force 11.*

Leo was in the pilothouse, grappling with the wheel. He must have glanced at his watch, because he remembered that it was two-thirty in the afternoon.

"Someone hollered there was a big sea coming. Some ran for the fo'c'sle and got below, some for the rigging, some for the pilothouse. It was as high as the mainmast. When it crashed down, I was washed along the deck and picked myself up by the dories on the lee side. I was floundering in the water, and as far as I knew I was overboard, but when it drained away, I was still on deck."

Henry Abbott and his tall dorymate Titus Wamboldt were trying to take in the riding sail.

"That sea, you could hear it roarin' long before it got to us. You could see it way up, musta been easily forty feet. Titus an' me jumped fer the riggin', half a dozen of us, an' up the shrouds. The heft of the sea went back against the mainmast an' turned her right around. That's how I got on the lee side. Some force o' water! I was up to the crosstrees at my head, an' my legs was in the water, she was that hove down. That lee riggin' was all slack an' shakin' so's it almost knocked me off. We hung on fer dear life. All I could see was the white bulwarks, way underneath the water, shinin'."

The men in the rigging were spared because the sea hit just below them. The dories were spared because it struck aft of them. It smashed down on the pilothouse full force and drove the weather wall down on Jack Dort and Manuel Marshall,

---

* For years Leo was haunted by the suspicion that it might have been safer to take in canvas earlier and jog under power. Probably not, he concluded. She didn't have enough power, unassisted by sail, to keep her head to that much wind.

Leo's old pal and faithful bos'n, Tom Bambury, rests on his fish fork only long enough for a glance at the camera. JOHN CLAYTON PHOTO

cracking Jack's ribs and injuring Manny's right arm and leg. Bos'n Tom Bambury was banged around. German Porter, crouching, grabbed the wheel and kept himself from being carried overboard.

The skipper was washed fifty feet up the deck and broke several ribs. The wall of water scooped up the shattered pilothouse, wrenched it from the eight iron tie rods (each 1¼ inches in diameter) that bolted it through the deck, and swept it over the side with Bill Nolan and Alex Muise.

From his perch in the rigging Henry Abbott caught a flash of Nolan, who must have been knocked unconscious, sixty feet out in the water.

"I could see Billy Nolan with his oil jacket on when there was a break in the sea, 'cause after it hit her it was right calm an' smooth an' all froth, big bunches o' froth. He was drownded then, had his hands an' legs out. I s'pose it was the wind, the air, in his oilskins kep' him afloat."*

Alex Muise was a younger man, thirty-five, nine years younger than Billy

* That strange, ghastly calm reminded Abbott of "how we dragged [lay to a drag, or sea anchor] the dories when adrift. If you put over a trawl tub an' let it go ahead fifty or sixty foot an' slack yerself back in the dory, no matter how big the sea is, when it comes to that tub it'll break."

Nolan. He was a Novie who had fished most of his life out of Gloucester, never bothered to learn to swim. They could see him from the rigging and the deck in those few moments before they collected themselves. He was clinging to the top of the pilothouse. Someone threw him a rope with a noose in the end, but he seemed too badly hurt to grab it, and *Adventure* drifted out of reach.

Leo had limped back to the wheel, which was as naked to the weather now as the day the vessel was launched, and put his helm hard over to make as tight a circle as they could to come back up to Alex for another try. There wasn't the faintest chance of getting a dory overboard to go after him in those seas without swamping.

*Adventure **pulls away from the Boston Fish Pier, throttling down for a portrait taken by John Clayton around 1950. Logan Airport and the twentieth century are across the harbor. On the old schooner, the fore gaff, the jumbo boom, the jib, and the familiar main topmast hardware are gone. The swordfish pulpit is pulled up and out of the way. The Old Lady still carries twelve dories and two spares. The skipper's famous spot buoy leans high against the pilot house. His air horn is clamped to the engine stack. Big ventilators have been added for the living quarters and engine room. As a rule, Leo kept the mainsail and foresail up to steady her in a seaway and to add some speed when the wind was fair. He rarely used the headsails. Often while fishing he would cut the engine and jog under sail alone.** JOHN CLAYTON PHOTO*

The Lionhearts 103

The plunging schooner came up again on the oilskinned figure clutching the edge of the wreckage. They shouted above the storm and tossed him the line, but he just seemed too far gone to catch it. They hauled it back and tried again, and this time he got it—except that now they were ranging ahead, past him, past him, pulling, pulling on the rope.

His man was so close that Leo could touch his oil jacket, yet they couldn't get a hand on him. The skipper in desperation signaled Fred Thomas to throw the engine in reverse, but it stuck in neutral. There was water in the engine room. Something was wrong down there. Abbott watched in helpless horror.

"Leo figgered he could have gone back on him, drifted down on him, but the engine stuck on center. He give her the bells, an' goddammit, I can see it now, the engine went SHHHHH SHHHHH. I can see it now—the exhaust pipe, the black smoke comin' out. An' then the man let go the rope, the vessel goin' ahead. That was an awful thing."

They circled. There was nothing but bits of wreckage.

For twenty more hours her men worked to keep *Adventure* afloat as the near-hurricane roared across the sea. The next day, the fourteenth of March, the third straight day of it, the storm began to blow itself out, and they pumped their way home, flag once again at half-mast, this time for Billy Nolan, father of three, and Alex Muise, father of two.*

Half wrecked, the Old Lady pulled into the Fish Pier on the fifteenth, Wednesday, the early morning sun at her back. The twisted tie rods, where the pilothouse had been, stuck up incongruously around the wheelbox.

A Boston newspaper reporter brought the word to Billy Nolan's widow in East Boston, and her reaction back to his readers.

"It seems just too terrible to be true. I don't know how I'll tell the children. Vera is nine, Marie seven, and Junior five. They go to Fitton School of Holy Redeemer Church parish. They'll be home this afternoon. Then they'll have to know.

"I haven't had time yet to plan how I'll take care of them. I'll have to get a job. That will be the first thing. We haven't any relatives nearer than Newfoundland. My husband and I were just getting on our feet financially. He was sick and in the hospital a year and a half ago. He hoped this fishing trip would give us a stake. I hated to see him go. But it wasn't any use protesting.

"I hate the sea anyway. It's cruel, cruel, cruel!"

* The blizzard was the worst of the winter. Ernest Parsons was bringing the *Lark* home to Boston from Browns Bank when the Channel Express was hit by a sea that tore off the after end of the pilothouse and slammed one of the crew around inside, badly injuring him. The *Gertrude L. Thebaud* was on Browns too. Captain Cecil Moulton heard the weather forecast and ran up the Bay of Fundy trying to make Yarmouth when she was struck by eighty-knot winds. While she was hove-to, a crashing sea inundated the *Thebaud* fore and aft, ripped the wooden hoops to which the riding sail was bent clean off the mainmast, and smashed the pilothouse windows. Luckily, the crew had ducked below or into the house, and no one was hurt.

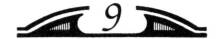

War Comes to Adventure

Hark! The hunt turns 'gainst the hunter—
The fish upon the fisherman.

Anonymous

Germany invaded Poland on September 1, 1939, and launched a world war for the second time in twenty-five years. For the second time in a single generation, very little in the self-styled civilized world would ever be the same again.

As America's nominal neutrality gave way to mounting support of the Allies, the Battle of the Atlantic stepped up in 1940 and 1941. German submarines and pocket battleships inflicted alarming losses on Allied and neutral shipping, culminating in attacks on American destroyers doing convoy duty west of Iceland in October 1941, two months before the bombing of Pearl Harbor.

Since the founding of the Republic, the fisheries had been considered the "nursery" of the Navy, and soon after the Japanese attack, it was drafting the pick of the North Atlantic fishing fleet for patrol duty until the shipyards could get geared up.

The Coast Guard decreed that no enemy aliens could go fishing, which beached many Italians. They then pronounced that aboard dory trawlers the captain, engineer, cook, and at least one man per dory must be a citizen, which beached numerous patriotic Canadians. And then there was the draft, exchanging G.I. and SNAFU for oilskins and fog.

These wartime strictures resulted in the mass conversion of dory trawlers to dragging, which required less than half the crew and less equipment. The *Gertrude L. Thebaud*, for example, wound up on Atlantic patrol duty as much because half the crew was not American as because she was Queen of the Fleet. A wonder that any at all were able to hew to the old ways.

Adventure did. By 1941 she was fifteen, over draft age for a wooden vessel, manned predominantly by Yankees—both native and whitewashed—and under Captain Hynes, now forty-one, one of the highline producers of the fleet. And Uncle Sam needed fish.

Before Pearl Harbor, *Adventure* displayed American flags painted prominently on each side of the bow to identify her as a neutral fishing off the coast of combatant Canada. After the Japanese attack the government ordered the flags and the rest of the hull painted over with battleship gray. Leo and the other skippers were designated "confidential obeservers" by the Navy, under instructions to report anything unusual seen at sea, such as more than three planes in formation and signs of submarines.

In an encore of the finale of World War I, German U-boats by 1942 were hitting fishing vessels, sporadically, just to get the message across in the international language of violence that the underwater enemy didn't take to the unexpected possibility of prying eyes whenever he popped up his periscope.

In a gesture that probably sounded good at the time, the Navy established a submerged but movable Maginot Line across the main channel of Boston Harbor. This was a buoyed chain-link steel net that would supposedly prevent a U-boat from sneaking into the chicken coop, or detect if if it tried. The "gate" was drawn every night like a theatre curtain, opened every morning at a certain hour to let the fishermen pass out to their grounds at their own risk. This Rube Goldberg rig between Deer and Long islands was a nuisance to the fishermen, if not to the Germans, especially to In-and-Out Hynes.

"If we came back to Boston in the evening, they wouldn't let us past, and we had to wait outside for the signal next morning. One time we were all bunched up around Graves Light, sparring for position to get the signal first and get in to the Fish Pier first for the top price. This beam trawler, the *Newton*, come up full speed and plowed right into us on the quarter. Turned the whole rail in from by the pilothouse right up to the break, broke the stanchions off, and we had to lose a trip for repairs. I called the skipper all the sons o' bitches!"

Contrariwise, Henry Abbott recalled that the gate served as the occasion of a Blessed Wartime Event at sea, courtesy of *Adventure*'s mascot. "One night we were comin' home an' failed to make the submarine gate, an' while we was joggin', waitin',

Skippy had puppies, four or five of the prettiest little things, white as snow. Poor dog, moanin' an' groanin', and I can hear Leo now, 'What's the matter, Skip, what's the matter?'"

The unseen presence of German raiders prowling off the coast, and the surface evidence alone of their underhanded deeds, made fishing a decidedly unpleasant game of cat and mouse.

The mouse, one moonlit June night in 1944, was none other than the schooner *Lark*, *Adventure*'s old rival, now under Jimmy Abbott of *Thebaud* fame while Ernest Parsons was off beam trawling. They were steaming along on the fishing grounds when an unfriendly submarine broke the surface about a hundred yards off, fired a shot from its cannon across their bow, and machine-gunned the sails and rigging. All the crew but Abbott, Dan Maloney, the seventy-four-year-old cook, and the ship's dog, Rex, took to the dories. The U-boat disappeared—for good, thought the skipper— but before the trio on board could get another dory over, it materialized again and poured eight shells and a hail of machine-gun fire into the old schooner.

The skipper dashed about the deck, dodging shot and shell, and after the U-boat ceased fire and submerged for good, evidently supposing the victim would soon enough sink, he found his cook down below, dressed in his shore clothes and preparing to abandon ship as cool as you please.

After a while one of the dories some distance away returned, and they all got the engine going. *Lark* picked up the rest, and with all back on board, they pumped their leaking old schooner home to Boston and a hero's welcome for the skipper, the cook, and the dog.*

About seven American fishing vessels were sunk by German subs in the Battle of the Atlantic—enough to give the jitters to the rest, and Leo Hynes was no exception.

"After the *Lark* everybody got kinda worried, and we used to follow the shore. A fleet of us left Boston and followed along to Mount Desert and across Fundy to Yarmouth. But I got a little bit bold, knew it was gonna be fine the next day, and cut out and fished on Cashes. The moon was coming up one night, and we thought we saw a submarine, so we changed course and went up north for a couple of hours. Always blacked out, of course. The same night a sub did attack on the surface and shot up a ship. Coupla men killed."

Another time *Adventure* passed a scattering of lifejacketed bodies off Cape Cod and learned over the radio that three American ships had been sunk that night. Soon after, they encountered an empty fifty-man lifeboat too big to lift on deck with the dory tackles, try as they might, and too much to tow.

Adventure's men got their worst scares not from the enemy's subs but from the organized efforts of their friends and allies to protect themselves from the wolf pack, namely, the convoys steaming out of Halifax and St. John, New Brunswick,

* Less than a year later, in May 1945, as the war was ending in Europe, *Lark* sailed from Gloucester for Tahiti in her second career as a French freighter in the South Seas.

for Europe—hundreds of freighters, tankers, troopships, and their naval escorts, right across the fishing grounds. Like crossing Fifth Avenue against the traffic lights. It made Leo nervous.

"We were on Browns, had the dories out for the morning set. One parted the trawl, and they rowed out and hauled away from all the rest. Well, I could see this convoy coming and thought we had time. The corvettes were out ahead, scouting. They had sonar. I got 'em all aboard except this one dory that was about three miles off. The next thing, this corvette darted out and started laying down depth charges. The water was going way the hell up in the air, and not far from the dory. So I steamed up to him as fast as we could go, and they were still hauling their trawl!

"I said, 'For God's sake, cut it off!' The two jumped up on the stern of the *Adventure* with the painter, and I towed that dory away as fast as I could, two or three miles from that convoy, before we hoisted it in. We didn't fish any more that day. I took off for Yarmouth!"

*The knockabout schooner **Mary P. Goulart**, looking remarkably like Adventure— a descendant of hers for whom she, in an ironic turn, later would be named—sails into Gloucester almost down to her scuppers with fish from a trip dory trawling. All sail, no power. The date is April 21, 1912, and the future Adventure II is no more than a year old, having been built in Gloucester in 1911. The diamond shape near her bow may be a chafe plate for the anchor stock.* EBEN PARSONS PHOTO, AUTHOR'S COLLECTION

The next encounter was closer.

"We were down on the western side of Sable Island Bank, still had three tubs out, and I looked and here was this convoy coming, ships everywhere! And I said, 'For God's sake, get it in as fast as you can! We gotta cross in front of that convoy and get beyond 'em!' Couple of the fellers parted their trawls off, and we got delayed, and my God, what a time we had to get through those ships! Dark overtook us, and they weren't carrying any lights, and we weren't. I never thought we'd survive it."

The third was the worst.

"We were near Cape Sable, and I knew there was gonna be an old sou'wester, it was getting that thick, so I decided to cut across Browns Bank. By God, around ten o'clock that night we landed right in a convoy from St. John! Wherever we went there was ships. They towed something behind them when the water was firing, phosphorescent, so they could see each other. Well, we put the dories in the slings and put on our lifejackets, all of us on deck, ready to drop 'em over in case there was a collision.

"We finally saw one ship, a big hull looming up outta the fog, and we turned around and went with him, and after a while a corvette came up, and they hollered over to us and told us how to get outta there. Hundreds of vessels it musta been, and no lights. Christ, everybody was scared, myself included."

Back before the war, in 1938, Leo Hynes had handed *Adventure* over to Captain Frank Mitchell while he took a leave to try his luck as skipper of the large beam trawler *Boston College*. After she was tied up by a strike, he and Phil Manta bought the ancient Gloucester dory trawler *Mary P. Goulart* at auction for $10,000.* The *Goulart* was a little smaller than *Adventure* and more than a little the worse for wear, having been fished since 1911. They spent a few thousand to spruce her up and renamed her *Adventure II*. On September 19, 1938, Captain Hynes took her on her first trip under her new name and ownership down to his old haunt, the South Channel. Parsons was down there too, in the *Lark*.

"We had started to make our second set when I saw Parsons steaming north without making his. You could tell from the feel of it that something was up. We didn't have the radiotelephone then, so I went below and turned on the radio. The weather report would scare you to death!"

You bet it would scare you to death, such as it was. Hynes and Parsons were lucky they had any advance warning at all. This was the infamous 1938 hurricane approaching, the worst natural disaster ever recorded as hitting the Atlantic coast, the worse because it was virtually unpredicted.

"I went around to all the dories to get 'em in, which took the better part of

* The *Mary P. Goulart* was built in Gloucester and sailed out of there until some time after World War I, when she was sold down to Provincetown. She was 119 tons gross, 66 net, 104 feet on the waterline, 24 beam, ten feet nine inches deep. Fitted with a 180-h.p. diesel when Hynes and Manta first had her, she was pretty slow compared with *Adventure*'s 230-h.p. engine.

three hours, and then headed for home. When we were about off Nauset, the riding sail blew away and a sea came over the cabin house and knocked the skylight off. We had to heave-to and stop the engine and start pumping. It was blowing sixty or seventy by then, no'theast, and we were drifting toward Nauset Beach. I figgered we'd get close in and then start the engine and hold her off long enough that maybe some of the fellers would be saved.

"Well, the wind moderated right then and backed around for a while to the sou'west, and we were able to keep off and make it into Provincetown before the full force of it. After that, I gave [the command of] *Adventure II* to Mike O'Hearn and went back to *Adventure*."

Four years and a few months passed, and America was in the middle of the war. General Seafoods Corporation of Boston, owner of a fleet of steel draggers and a pioneer in quick-freezing, was building up a fleet down in Florida to bring in fruit from Cuba in the early spring of 1943 and offered the partners $27,000 for *Adventure II*, a deal they could hardly refuse—after one more trip. It was the middle of March.

Her namesake was still out when *Adventure* pulled away from the Fish Pier about two in the afternoon of March 20. Leo had the helm. It was foggy as they felt their way through the channel, and when they approached The Graves, they found that the submarine gate was closed. They hove-to with a growing fleet of fishermen until just before sundown, when it scaled up somewhat, and with the improved visibility, the gate was opened and they streamed through. But they were hardly outside, with the prospect of having to thread their way through a convoy that was making up, when it came in thick again.

Henry Abbott had been topside and thought he'd slip down to his bunk in the main cabin for a quick flake, since nothing was happening on deck.

" 'Twas a beautiful night, a lovely night, only thing it was foggy. Goin' out the harbor, it was so calm an' nice, and damn if the fog didn't shut right down, black thick o' fog. Leo was lookin' at the glass, an' he says, 'Jeez Chris', the glass is startin' to jump crazy, what the hell is gonna happen?' So he went forrard, an' they were playin' cards, they had a lotta liquor, all drinkin'.

"Steamin', black thick o' fog, horn goin'. Not many of us aft, an' I got in the bunk, an' 'Jeez Chris' I heard this yellin' an' screechin', an' I could look up an' see Leo spinnin' the wheel. Then I could feel her when she started goin' up, an' then come down. I was outta my bunk, had my boots in my hand!"

Leo had no sooner steered *Adventure* clear of the convoy and all the confusing engine sounds in the fog and descending dark, pumping regularly on his air whistle, when all of a sudden—as it so often happens at sea in the thick—two horn blasts erupted close aboard to starboard.

"I spun the wheel hard over to port, and the next thing we knew, this vessel come out of the fog right across our bow and WHAM, we hit 'em in the stern and the whole stern collapsed.

The Mary P. Goulart *ambles along, possibly in Boston Harbor in the 1930s.*
By this time the jib, foresail, and mainsail have been traded in for an
engine, a big stack with a big "G" and an air horn, a ventilator, and a pilot
house—practically all the comforts and conveniences. SHARP COLLECTION

"By God, it was *Adventure II* coming back from her trip! They had stopped their engine and blowed two blasts, which means you're supposed to be stopped, but they didn't think about their momentum, and they were probably going six or seven knots."

Henry Abbott was on deck in a flash.

"We cut her in two. Course we were light, just goin' out, an' she had a trip o' fish an' was heavy an' was an old vessel, an' we rode our bow right up onto her. All you could hear aboard of her was men screechin', trying to git in the dories, an' there was half of the vessel floatin' away, an' on the other side of us, there was the other half.

"An' when she started to go down—it was thirteen minutes—her bow was right up in the air, an' all you could see was fish goin' in the air, them haddock goin' up like rubber balls, the water goin' SSSSSHHHH! The bulkheads was busted, an' the pressure of the water was drivin' the fish up."

Captain Mike O'Hearn had turned the helm of *Adventure II* over to a Portuguese fisherman whose English was pretty limited. O'Hearn:

"We had a port list, and *Adventure* come out of the fog and hit us on the port side just behind the mainmast. I was up on deck blowing the horn, and we were stopped. *Adventure* broke through behind the main rigging, broke the timbers and opened up the engine room. It's kind of an open place there with nothing to give her lateral strength.

"My engineer was out in a dory. 'Come on, Mike,' he shouts, 'she's goin' and goin' quick!' And I got in the dory. We lost everything. No one had time to pick up any personal gear at all. If she had hit a little bit farther forward, the mast would have come down and probably would have hurt some of the crew around on deck. As it was, everyone got off safely. She went down stern first, blowed like a whale! I can still hear the sound."

Henry Abbott had run forward to the dories.

"We got our dories out on both sides. Two or three of the men was in the water an' hung on to the sterns of 'em. One ole fella from the other vessel, Muckle Bill, a Frenchman, was so big an' heavy we tried to git him in over the stern o' the dory, but it hurt his stomach so, we tole him to hold on an' towed him aboard."

Muckle Bill had brought his plight on himself. He was already in one of *Adventure II*'s dories when he remembered his false teeth in his bunk in the fo'c'sle. They rowed him back, and he clambered aboard his sinking ship and went down and retrieved them. But just as he struggled back up on deck she took the plunge, and he found himself thrashing around in the drink.

It was the closest call Henry Abbott ever saw, that collision.

"Well, we started back for Boston and wasn't turned around fifteen minutes when it hit like that, SMACK, from the nor'west. Man, you couldn't stand on deck! A regular hurricane, it got rough so quick, but soon enough we got into smoother water.

"An' down below in the cabin after we got in, Leo an' Mike Dempsey, as we called O'Hearn, got arm-rasslin'. They usta be always rasslin' an' carryin' on. An' Leo throwed Mike, an' his legs went up an' hit the stove, an' knocked it down, an' there was the stove an' coals all over, an' it's a wonder we didn't catch fire."

So they lost *Adventure II*, formerly the schooner *Mary P. Goulart*, age thirty-two years, and 85,000 pounds of fish worth $10,000 at the Fish Pier. She was insured for $10,000, which was $17,000 less than their deal with General Seafoods that got deep-sixed in the bargain. The crew sued for the personal gear that went down with her. *Adventure* had to be hauled for repairs.

For all that, the war year of 1943 was the biggest *Adventure* ever had. They made forty-seven trips and stocked $364,000, which is more than likely some kind of a record for a dory trawler.

All in all, an unlucky, and mighty lucky encounter in a black thick o' fog, and an unlucky, and mighty lucky year.

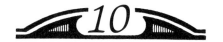

The Old Lady's Boys

Well, I'll say one thing for the Depression. It brought the rest of the world down to the level of the fishermen.

Captain Bill Sibley of Gloucester

hen Captain Hynes went forward in *Adventure* with some order cloaked as a suggestion, or for a consultation or just a visitation, he would stamp noisily on the companionway steps as he descended to alert the gang in case they were talking among themselves. His custom spoke volumes of the relationship between master and men in a New England fishing vessel.

There has never been anything quite like it. The give-and-take, the assumption of equality, the tacit recognition of command, the mutual restraint — all are old Yankee to the core. Thus the colonial militia conducted their affairs and their campaigns — and the farmers, the lumberjacks, the volunteer firefighters, the road makers, barn raisers, and boatbuilders. The maintenance of that subtle balance may have been most to the point with the fishermen.

The fishermen signed on together, sailed, ate, drank, slept, raised hell, cut bait, fished, fought the elements, endured, shared, and drowned together, captain and crew. There was none of that physical and psychological separation between

Astride land and sea, Captain Leo Hynes navigates the lives and fortunes of his twenty-six adventurers. JOHN CLAYTON PHOTO

officers and men that reigned on merchant and naval vessels, braid and the quarter-deck versus bare feet and the brig. The skipper of *Adventure* occupied the main cabin because the helm and the compass were within reach, and he shared it with his bos'n, his engineer, and as many of his men as could squeeze in. The cabin was separated from the galley and the fo'c'sle by the fishhold, which in every other way bound all on board together and was their reason for being there.

No fishing skipper could succeed except with respect and results. Yet ability and authority were as nothing in such a wholly cooperative venture when dependent upon men who were hostile, lazy, or incompetent. A crew was not committed to one vessel or one skipper for more than a trip at a time, but a site with the highline

Newfoundlander Henry Allen, the skipper's brother-in-law and an old-time dory fisherman, coils trawl aft of the break. Hook-set on the tub, box of hooks on the hatch, dory hook slipped into the eye on the rail just ahead of the main rigging. Henry wears several turns of brass chain around his wrists in the belief that the vertigris, or corrosion therefrom, counteracts the effect of the salt water on the skin opened up by the constant chafing of the oilskin cuffs, which frequently produces sores and pimples on the wrists and forearms. Various such wrist bands of one material or another were favored by the dorymen. JOHN CLAYTON PHOTO

captains in the top vessels (and the two gravitated to each other) was a prize to hang on to. During the Depression years of the 1930s, good men haunted the Boston and Gloucester waterfronts for a berth with such as Hynes and Parsons, eager for the greater risks with the drivers who were in and out fast and fished hard in all weather on the treacherous spots where the fish gathered — top dollar (for what it was worth) for one and all.

"A thankless profession," writes Jack Olson, who grew up in Gloucester. His father, Steve Olson, a Swedish immigrant, was lost with his dorymate from the *Oretha F. Spinney* fishing off Newfoundland on March 7, 1935. "It took a special breed of person to do this work. It is a horrible life, as the seas can get real mean. Being in a compartment where they live is intolerable. Each member of the crew has different ideas of entertainment. Some play cards when they aren't fishing, some have radios playing full blast, others make other noises, then some want to sleep and get rest in a smoke-filled compartment. That is hell, and that's putting it mildly. They all take watch, and are at the wheel when their turn comes. They must be alert at all times.

"The big terror they had is when it was foggy. They were afraid of big ocean liners, freighters, warships or any large boat ramming them. If this happened, they wouldn't have a chance to survive. If a man or men were lost at sea, they would get their share of the trip and that was all. The widow and survivors had to shift for themselves. My father didn't believe in life insurance, so when his share of the trip was spent, that was it."

Especially among the dory trawlers, risks could bring rewards of sorts for the strongest and the most courageous. Worth it, perhaps, with a Leo Hynes who pretty consistently beat the odds with daring tempered by experience, intuition, and always the factor of fisherman's luck. Long-time observers of In-and-Out Hynes and his breed, however, sensed that luck on the water could be as weighted as ashore in a laboratory — it was, after all, scientist Louis Pasteur's assertion that chance favors the prepared mind.

For such a mix between fore and aft, the cliché *motley crew* begs literal application.

Quiet, competent Tom Bambury, Leo's bos'n for most of the time since they sailed together from their native Newfoundland with salt fish for Portugal in 1919, was eleven years his skipper's senior and missed a trip for nothing short of an emergency.

It was the cook, however, who, next to the captain, was the leading functionary aboard and by universal acclamation or condemnation, as the case might be, the hardest working. Of the three or four who reigned at one time or another in *Adventure*'s smoky and grease-stained galley during the Hynes era, the most striking was the last, Pat Nolan, inevitably known, for the gleam of his pate, as Paddy the Wig. "If there's a hair in the soup, it ain't mine."

Chef extraordinaire, Paddy (the Wig) Nolan peers into his coffee pot while yet another mess of grub simmers on his stove. JOHN CLAYTON PHOTO

Nolan jumped ship from *Lark* to *Adventure* in 1948 at the age of sixty-eight. He started fishing at thirteen from his native island of St. Pierre, a provenance that belied his name, and had gone cook nearly half a century on merchant ships and fishing vessels. "A hard life, but not too bad."

The Old Lady's Boys 117

Up on the fo'c'sle table, Leo Romaine gets out the big model of **Adventure** *he's been building between sets.* JOHN CLAYTON PHOTO

A hard life, all right. Up all hours of the day and night slinging the chow for twenty-six eager eaters, two sittings a meal, a man from each dory at a time wolfing it down while his mate stayed on deck baiting up. Baking bread, biscuits, pies, and cookies, frying doughnuts on the big black cookstove, two kinds of meat every meal, peeling spuds, chopping vegetables, Pat Nolan summoned them to mess with a shrill shriek on his police whistle, dealt out the plates around the fo'c'sle table from his stack, poker-fashion. For a starter, six eggs and the fixings were required every morning for the skipper, who never got over the habit of gulping it all down in ten minutes.

The cook's job on a dory trawler demanded indomitability and versatility, for which in return he earned the right to irascibility. Paddy was a crotchet, and with ample reason. Even in the heat of summer his stove consumed four baskets of wood and a ton of coal a trip, the ice box a ton of ice. After washing and wiping all the dishes ("Old Pat would wipe a few dishes and then wipe under his arms," expostulated his captain. "Honest! I caught him!"), the ruler of the galley had to tote all his garbage and dirty water topside and dump it over the rail.

One winter morning they were coming into Shelburne, all iced up, when Paddy the Wig emerged on deck to blow his breakfast whistle, slipped, and knocked himself out. They revived him, and he went back to his galley and served out two sittings.

Besides having bounce, the cook on fishing vessels was expected to be on hand to help get the dories out and in, and when a set was finished, to pitch in on deck with the culling of the catch, and to be an expert enough mariner to take over the vessel if anything befell the skipper while the dories were out or simply whenever called upon. In former times his alleged medical skills were occasionally called upon, and he was referred to as the "doctor." In 1949 *Adventure*'s cook was paid about twenty-five dollars a trip in addition to his share.

Pat Murphy was Paddy the Wig's predecessor, and the cook while Henry

It may be a mess, but it's home away from home. This rare photograph of a schooner's forecastle reveals the massive, bolted shelf tying Adventure's deck beams to the frames behind the ceiling, above the cramped upper bunks. Farther up in the bow, tapering down through the deck, is the pawl post, main strength of the windlass, with the bitt at the head of the table; it sets right down into the keel and also takes the jumbo stay. JOHN CLAYTON PHOTO

The Old Lady's Boys   119

Frank Mayo, doryman first, lady's man second. Close-up of ground line, gangings, and hooks. The stern becket of the topmost dory in the nest, secured with Matthew Walker knots, is enclosed in canvas chafing gear where the burton tackle hook grabs, while the next down is served with marline. JOHN CLAYTON PHOTO

Abbott was in the crew. "Comical. A great cook. Oh, that bread had that crust on it! He couldn't make a bad batch o' bread. Melt in yer mouth! An 'boy, did he swear if they left the skylight open and a sea come down on his stove!"

Crotchety too. On one trip, *Adventure* had sailed into Liverpool, Nova Scotia, for bait. When it came time to get underway, Pat Murphy was the straggler, having hoisted a few, and he suggested to Captain Leo that he'd come aboard when he was good and ready. "So I took the vessel out over the bar at the entrance to the harbor and hove-to. Old Pat was there on the beach. I sent a dory ashore and told 'em, 'If he don't wanna get in that dory, you come on back and t'hell with him.' He got in the dory."

Old Pat Murphy was an advanced diabetic and suffered the amputation of both legs. That was the end of his seacooking days. A third cook, Ronald Gillis, a big, stout Newfie and likewise a distinct individualist, knew his stuff and was with *Adventure* for some time.

A fourth cook put one over on Leo Hynes once, but not twice. *Adventure* was up on the railway at Lunenburg for repairs during a freeze that was so severe the cradle stuck and they couldn't let her back down. Meanwhile, the skipper gave this old character a bonus of five dollars a week to keep the boys well fed and happy while they weren't fishing and making any money. The cook supposedly ordered the extra grub from a former dorymate who had a grocery store up on the hill, which was all right with Leo until some time later he ran across a bill for 126 dozen eggs that, as he discovered upon further investigation, had not yet even been laid — it turned out it was all going for red rum.

As diesel power insinuated itself between the main cabin and the fishhold of the schooners, the man in charge of the throbbing heart took his place behind the cook in the offhand hierarchy aboard. In *Adventure* this meant William-Felix Thomas, engineer when his cousin Jeff launched her in 1926, still engineer almost to the day that Leo Hynes called it quits twenty-seven years and three engines later, at a share and fifteen dollars a trip.

They came and they went, but Fred Thomas stayed on and grew old in the service of the schooner that bridged the ages of sail and power, a gnarled and grouchy mascot. Old Fred in his turn, besides his engine, had charge of his canine counterpart, Skippy, a nondescript, mongrelish-toward-the-chow, crosspatch of a sea dog. The three of them — the old vessel, the old bachelor, and the old bitch — occupied inseparably their niche in the waterfront lore from Boston to Bay l'Argent.

Like the rest of the Thomases, Fred was born in Arichat. He went fishing when he was twelve and must have arrived in the States while still young, because his first site, at sixteen, was aboard Captain Maurice Whalen's fast plumb-stem schooner, the famed *Harry L. Belden*. Six years earlier, in August 1892, the *Belden* had beaten the fabled *Nannie C. Bohlin* in the first of the formal fishermen's races off Gloucester, "The Race that Blew," which was sailed in a near-hurricane.

A common sailor all his life, but a master of tall stories, Leo (Big Mac) MacDonald can turn his hand to most anything around a vessel, including the caulking of a bottom seam of his dory, for which no fancy caulker's mallet is required. JOHN CLAYTON PHOTO

Fred was rail-thin in his later years but hadn't always been so. In his prime, they said, he topped two hundred pounds, until the day, while with Jeff, that he came up from the heat of the engine room to the cool fresh air on deck, got a chill, came down with pneumonia, and was never the same again after he left the hospital.

Like Murphy the cook, he was diabetic and had to find new territory twice a day for his insulin shots.

To his latter-day mates Fred was an ailing, lonely, justifiably cranky old bach, and they stayed clear of his cussedness. He conversed with his engine, as his skipper admired, and it purred right back to him, and he kept his machinery, his engine room, his bunk in the main cabin across from Leo's, his duds, and himself spotless. Scrub, scrub, scrub, always scrubbing the four walls and the beating pulse

Engineer Fred Thomas orchestrates the 230 horses of his Cooper-Bessemer diesel. JOHN CLAYTON PHOTO

of his life, but when Fred was in his Toscanini mood while tuning her up, duck: the wrenches flew around like batons from the podium.

Some time around 1936, early in the Hynes regime, Skippy turned up to brighten Fred Thomas's life. She was only a pup and wandered one day into the carpenter's shop down on the Fish Pier, where she slept in the shavings and begged for food. *Adventure* was about to leave for a trip when she came down on the wharf, jumped aboard, trotted right down aft to the engine room, and adopted Fred. From that day on, the schooner was Skippy's doghouse and the crew her privileged guests.

Skippy soon recognized the steps of all twenty-seven of the two-legged creatures she allowed on board, but let a stranger set foot on deck and she would tear up the gangway to snap at the trespasser and drive him off. In her dotage, though, it was observed that the vicious snarl and baring of doughnut-worn teeth were more for show, and she could be outbluffed by a strong personality.

In her self-appointed guard duties Skippy had the assistance, for a time, of a retired fisherman who served as night watchman between trips. The old gent slept in the galley and set metal pie plates on the gangway steps, with a fish fork handy. One of the crew stumbled aboard late one night, and into this makeshift alarm system, and almost got stuck. *Adventure*'s pie-plate alarm puts one in mind of Captain Joshua Slocum's sprinkling of carpet tacks on the deck of his immortal *Spray* to repel the fierce but barefooted Fuegians when they tried to board as he passed through the Strait of Magellan on his singlehanded circumnavigation in 1895.*

Skippy was useless in the face of four-legged boarders with pointed noses and pencil-thin tails. Rats would scamper from the Fish Pier up the docking lines and hide out in the chain box up forward. The men dumped boiling water into the box and tried to chase them back ashore with fish forks, with indifferent results. Unfortunately, the varmints developed a taste for the manila trawl-buoy lines. Once while they were fishing and the dories were out, one of the gang yelled up to Leo, "Hey, Cap, my buoy keg's come adrift!"

Skippy ate well if not always wisely, such as when a joker in the crew fed her a popular chocolate-covered laxative, which she so relished that he gave her the whole box, and thereafter she bit anyone she saw with a chocolate. She bathed well if unwillingly, every month whether she needed it or not, when Fred filled the bait jack (the half-barrel reserved normally for bait) with water—her signal to take refuge under the windlass. And she behaved well, if not always warily, except once when she was in heat. Hoping to prevent complications, her protector trussed her up, chastity-belt-fashion, with adhesive tape. But Skippy slipped ashore on one of her rare AWOLs and had her puppies anyway.

---

* Did he get the idea from John Babson's *History of Gloucester*, published thirty years earlier? Captain Andrew Robinson, builder of the first "scooner" at Gloucester in 1713, survived several narrow ones at the hands of Indians while sailing the New England coast, according to Babson, once by scattering broadheaded nails on deck, which enabled him to pitch the wildly hopping invaders back over the rail as soon as they boarded.

*One of the best, Jake Flores works deftly on a splice
back aft by the pilothouse.* JOHN CLAYTON PHOTO

The Old Lady's Boys 125

Cozily settled in the lee of the dories and out of the breeze,
Nova Scotian Peter Meuse overhauls his trawl. JOHN CLAYTON PHOTO

Mike O'Hearn, the big fisherman and sometime skipper they called Mike Dempsey for his peaceful nature, was eight years older than Leo Hynes and a Newfoundlander with even harsher beginnings. He had shipped as a doryman with Hynes in *Adventure* before he took *Adventure II* and they had their fratricidal encounter. Mike quit school to go fishing when he was nine. ("If you have figures you can do pretty good, and there was always somebody building a boat or a house, and you got ideas.") At eighteen, in 1910, he went to sea in a square-rigger out of St. John's carrying salt fish to Brazil, where they loaded sand for ballast, sailed to Barbados, dumped it for molasses, and returned to Newfoundland.*

* Fifty-eight years later, in 1968, Mike O'Hearn sailed the last trip of his career in the beam trawler *Massachusetts* out of Boston. He was seventy-six. "Beam trawling, you didn't have your own life in your hands. All you had to do was dress fish. A different life altogether. I was brought up to a hand line. I didn't understand them nets."

Mike was impressed with *Adventure*'s ability. She could stand up like a church, as the sailing fishermen used to say, to the worst the sea could dish up, even when she was staggering and topheavy with ice. "With all that pig iron, she had a good hold on the water. You couldn't upset her. She'd go down pretty low, but that pig iron would bring her back."

Having been down pretty low once himself, Mike Dempsey knew whereof he spoke. It was February of 1917. The young Newfie had arrived in Gloucester and signed on Captain Joe Mesquita's brand-new all-sail schooner, the *Joseph P. Mesquita*, Captain Peter Richards. They had been fishing on Roseway Bank off Shelburne, what they called the Cape Shore, when the glass and the mercury dropped, and a storm swept in on the tenth. The sails were so frozen aloft they couldn't get them down. Mike had just come off watch, leaving the skipper and Morris Norris on deck.

"I went forward and was pouring a cup of coffee and was gonna get a bite from the shack locker when she rolled over and went down and down and down! The next thing I realized, I was standing on the doors of the shack locker. I said, 'This can't be right!'

"There was a feller sitting by the stove having a bite, and when she hove down, the lids and the coal damper and everything, pots and pans, fell on top of him, all of it red hot. Coals came right out of the stove in his lap. But the water struck in so quickly down the gangway that he wasn't even burned, came down in one great rush and extinguished the coals! Vinnie Fagan said, 'Oh, she's gone, she's gone!' He was the only man said anything.

"Just before that sea struck, one of the men up on watch said to the other, 'Look, that wave's gonna break on us!' The other one said, 'Naw, it'll break before reaching here.' He was some wrong.

"When we got on deck, Captain Richards was on the gurry kid, afloat near us. We saw him wave to us. I guess a lot went through his mind at that time. The other feller was in the rigging near the crosstrees. He'd thought the mast was broke off, but when the vessel righted he came down the throat halyard. He got tangled up in a buoy line that was snarled into the halyard when he was almost down. The buoy kept swinging around and hitting him in the nose, and he was bleeding. We let him down to the deck.

"The first thing that we saw on deck was the anchor chain that had washed from the chain box across the foredeck. An old Frenchman in front of me reached out to grab the chain and said, 'Hey, give me a hand!' When he realized what he was trying to do he let go; all that chain overboard would have been pretty hard for a man to haul in. We had sixteen single dories, all griped down on deck, and they were all split to pieces and gone."

Captain Richards was drowned. Morris Norris, saved by being thrown into the rigging when she hove onto her beam ends, was badly hurt. Mainsail, foresail, fore boom, and fore gaff were swept away. Flag half-mast, the crippled *Mesquita* was towed into Liverpool, Nova Scotia, by the auxiliary schooner *Matthew S. Greer* of Gloucester.*

Sooner or later in every crew a maverick or two would turn up, and *Adventure's* was no exception, though the record was remarkably pacific over the years. It was the misfortune of amiable Mike O'Hearn to fall afoul of two such tough nuts one time. They were fellow Newfies, brothers who had served in the First World War, married and brought home English girls, then left them for the States and joined *Adventure*.

The brothers made a habit of coming aboard drunk and dukes up. The younger and smaller would pick the fight — "make the snowballs," as Leo put it, for the bigger and the bully of the two to throw. Poor Mike one evening got in the way of this combination and was cuffed so badly he couldn't go in the dory for two days. Said their skipper: "Most every trip the cops would be down after one of them for nonsupport, and he'd have to send a few bucks back to his wife. I got a little loaded once myself in Lunenburg and subdued him. Had to keep charge. Wanted the men to respect me. Finally had to get rid of 'em."

One who never intended any trouble was Leo (Big Mac) MacDonald. **Big Mac** was so grand of girth that Skipper Leo had a hard time finding anyone to go dorymate with him. Finally he teamed him up with Henry Abbott, who was such a good fellow he'd go with anyone. Trouble was, as the diplomatic master of the *Adventure* defined it, "when Big Mac got in the bow of the dory, rowing or hauling trawl, he'd put it way down and the stern way up, skewing all over the place. Anway, he didn't break any oars. He couldn't pull hard enough. He'd always be a quarter of a mile behind the rest. Poor old Henry. He was a pretty tolerant feller, slept in the next berth to Big Mac and had to crawl in over him. Don't know how he got any air in there."

Besides being a master raconteur, Big Mac MacDonald was a master rigger and handled the maintenance during the summer for extra pay, actually climbing aloft. After he retired from dory trawling he found a job as watchman on a barge, fell off the gangplank, and drowned.

A ship of lions. A third Leo was Leo Romaine, a strong, large-boned Novie who always had something for the folks back in Yarmouth when *Adventure* put in around that way. He had served time on what was commonly believed to be a bum rap and lived on board. His mates paid him a dollar a tub to work on their trawls for them. One of the best with a doryload of fish and two oars, a craftsman in the fo'c'sle with a ship model, swordfish swords, or cribbage boards, and staunchly loyal to his skipper.

And there was quiet Henry Allen, the skipper's brother-in-law, mastheadman

* It was a hard war for the great Smoky Joe. Only ten months later, on December 9, 1917, the *Joseph P. Mesquita*, launched at Essex on August 28, 1916, drove ashore in a gale at Whitehead, Nova Scotia, and broke up. Captain Joseph Cass and his crew of twenty were saved. On the following August 20, the Germans sank Captain Joe's *Francis J. O'Hara, Jr.*

on the Canadian champion *Bluenose* during the 1938 races with the *Thebaud*, British Navy man in the war. And wiseacre Tom Fowler, ever a quip and among the best. Joaquim Flores, an old Portagee, top doryman for almost sixty years. Frank Mayo from Provincetown, another first-rate fisherman, and ladies' man too, nicknamed, with wry admiration, The Pimp. Archie Hubbard, with *Adventure* for almost thirteen years: "When it comes to making you haul against the tide, Leo is a man-killer." John Martins, a compact Portuguese with Leo almost from the start. Baited twice as fast as the others, a neat and hard worker. And Lawrence Doucette, another Novie from around Yarmouth and the finest kind.

Last and least—but more or less first in the hearts of her shipmates— is Skippy, venerable and voracious, mascot of the Adventure *for fifteen years. Dennis Meuse offers a soon-to-be greedily snapped-up tidbit.* JOHN CLAYTON PHOTO

The Old Lady's Boys   129

And so many others over all those years.

In-and-Out Hynes was a driver all right. He made 'em put those dories over, good weather and bad. But he found fish, and he never lost a man astray.

"My men were good men in the old days, very professional, very proud of their gear. For a while, some of them came from a little village in the center of Portugal. What fishermen! It wasn't my ability we got a lot of fish. It was the men I carried. Every hook had to be just right. They had a little wooden ring on their finger to straighten 'em. Never any arguments among the men over who was catching more or less. They shared alike. Nobody ever noticed what the other feller was getting. One day one might catch more, another day another would. My God, I respected those men!"

Even where individuality was the norm, there was the occasional eyebrow-raiser, however.

"We were about to sail and one of the men didn't show up. There was another feller down on the Fish Pier, and I said, 'Do you wanna go?' He said, 'Sure, gimme a chance to go over to East Boston and get my clothes.' I said, 'All right, I'll wait an hour.'

"Well when he came aboard old *Adventure* he'd had a few, and he opened his suitcase, and he had a cat in it. All he had, didn't have any clothes. We had that cat about eight years. He said, 'Well, I went home, an' the cat was runnin' across the floor, an'. . . .' "

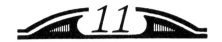

The Falling Curtain

Standing there at the wheel of the Adventure, *my thoughts kept roaming back into the past. Here was the very same wheel that my father had steered by so many times. Here was the last dory trawler, and the last schooner of her type in commission on this side of the Atlantic. Here was the very last of the beautiful schooners that I loved so much.*

Gordon Thomas, in *Fast and Able*

he First World War installed the engines in the schooners, which was the beginning of the end of them. The Second World War put all but the diehards to running winches, manhandling otter-trawl doors instead of dories over the rail, hauling back the big bag, the mixed bag, of creatures dragged up from the ocean floor, culling and cleaning night and day. Workers on a line.

By war's end in 1945, *Adventure* was one of a scattering of North Atlantic dory trawlers regarded by the rest of the fleet as oddities manned by an eccentric band of aging nostalgics too cranky to admit that the times had passed them by. Mighty hard worked, the battered old knockabout turned twenty in 1946. During the previous twelve years under Hynes she had more than held her own against the beam trawlers — "buckets of steel covered with ice" in the winter, scorned one of his loyal crew. But how much longer could the Old Lady and her old boys carry on against time and tide?

Adventure's jinx, if she had one, was the month of March, that fifth season so resented by New Englanders. Jeff Thomas died in March, Muise and Nolan were lost with the pilothouse in March, and she sank *Adventure II* in March.

On March 2, 1947, they had been fishing on Browns Bank when an easterly gale made up during the night, and Leo decided it was the better part of valor to run before it for home. All was well until she lurched into a sea that swung her head off and jibed the foresail, which came around with the crack of a thunderclap. The gaff struck the lee rigging and shattered, the end of it and the partially collapsed canvas whacking around and banging the shrouds with such abandon that it was only a matter of time before they parted. In that event, the strain on the foremast as *Adventure* rolled and pitched could snap it, and over the side with the mess, or it could put such a strain on the step as to open up the seams in her bottom.

The wind by now was blowing too hard to bring her up into it and haul down the sail and the fractured gaff from the deck, so Hynes himself climbed aloft, cut the twisted halyards, and dropped the tangle. Descending the ratlines, he just reached the light board when the schooner rolled and he saw a man tumble overboard and disappear. Such was the confusion in the storm that it was an hour before they could confirm that the missing man was Stanley Conrad, an experienced fisherman, sixty-two and the father of seven children.

And it was then that Conrad's ashen-faced dorymate remembered their last set before the gale, just before daylight. "We were hauling the trawl, and I saw this gull circling and circling around us all the time. That was the omen."

Home again, Leo took Lil with him to talk to the Conrad family in Cambridge, one of the hardest things he ever had to do. He felt like a criminal.*

No more chances. For the rest of her fishing days *Adventure* carried a gaffless leg-o'-mutton foresail.

She was getting tired, if not worn out.

There was that trip, bound for Browns, crossing Fundy with the tide against a forty-knot northeaster. Sharp, rolling head seas had *Adventure* pitching like a rocking horse, masts straining forward against the backstay when she punched into one, snapping back against the headstay as she recovered in the trough.

Not unexpectedly, you'd think, there was a mighty crack, and the mainmast-head broke off just above the hounds at the crosstrees, always a weak spot that attracts rain and rot in old spars. Down came ten or twelve feet of Oregon fir, sixteen inches thick at the broken base of it, which fetched up with a yank when the

---

* Years later Captain Hynes fell to talking one day with a couple named Brown who lived near one of his sons. "He said he was from Nova Scotia, and I asked him where his wife was from and her maiden name. It was Conrad, he said, and her father was lost with Leo Hynes on the *Adventure*. My God, I almost fell over! I had to go and meet his wife. She cried, and I said, 'I hope you're not resentful.'"

Tired but game, the Old Lady steams between the Boston Fish Pier and Commonwealth Pier, off on another trip in the early 1950s. She passes near the big beam trawlers that have all but put her on the shelf of history. JOHN CLAYTON PHOTO

springstay and the backstay shackled to the top caught on the crosstrees. Banging around up there with every lurch, this loose cannon aloft threatened to bring down the rest of the mast and all with it on their heads.

Running her off before it, the skipper had the men bend the main riding sail halyard, which was still intact from the mainmasthead, forward to the anchor chain, which they carried to the windlass and hove tight. Thus jury-rigged, with the broken mast secured and the masthead lashed to it, *Adventure* ran into Lunenburg for temporary orthopedic repairs.

It had to be a hell of a tight spot to make Leo Hynes cry uncle.

There was the leak, already described, that threatened to sink them coming home from Georges on April 20, 1948, when they pumped her back to Boston in the lee of the Coast Guard's 125-footer *General Greene*, which was hardly bigger than *Adventure*.

And there was the time Leo wished he hadn't asked for help. They were returning with a trip of fish from the South Channel when the engine broke down off Cape Cod near the Nauset buoy. Fred Thomas was stymied for once, so Leo got the Coast Guard on the radio, and the *General Greene* responded from Provincetown.

"He was towing us inside of Peaked Hill Bar buoy, and of course there's a ledge in there. He musta been a rookie. I got on the radio and shouted, 'For God's sake, you'll have us aground! We're drawing sixteen feet!' When he saw what he was doing, he turned right around and got us outta there, and another Coast Guard boat come up to tow us into Boston. The rookie come alongside in the *Greene* and said, 'Cap, I wish you hadn't got on the air. I'll get a reprimand for that.' I said, 'What didja expect me to do, go aground? I was desperate!'"

Alerted by *Adventure*'s near-sinking the previous year, the press by the spring of 1949 had rediscovered the once-taken-for-granted dory trawlers and was keeping a kind of death watch on the last of them, as if they were giant condors. John Bunker described the dying practice in the *Christian Science Monitor* of June 9, with a photograph of Captain Hynes, grizzled Ellsworth Buchanan, and Skippy in the pilothouse of one of the last of the kind out of New England. The other, the writer noted, was Captain Albert Hines's smaller *Marjorie Parker*. The third, the *Gertrude de Costa*, thirty-seven years of age, had just been auctioned out of fishing to Canadian parties.

How opportune that at this precise moment, just as the curtain was falling on dory trawling forever, along should come John Clayton. This enthusiastic, energetic, humorous, ever-curious advertising man from the West, a stickler for detail and an excellent amateur photographer, had become fascinated with the fading art of wooden shipbuilding, notably of the fishing schooners, when he happened on the last shipyards in Essex in the 1930s. Setting out to record every detail of the process, he took thousands of photographs, a selection of which was published in 1971 with an expository text by Dana A. Story, writer, historian, and boss of the Story yard, as *The Building of a Wooden Ship*.

By the end of the war *Adventure* was the most famous fishing schooner afloat, by 1949 one of the last two dory trawling. Clayton was determined to make a record before the curtain dropped. It didn't take much to persuade Leo Hynes to give him camera room aboard. On June 13, 1949, four days after Bunker's article appeared in the *Monitor*, John Clayton showed up at the Fish Pier for the first of the seven

Opposite: *Hauled out for regular repairs and painting at Gloucester around 1950,* **Adventure** *reveals her strong underwater lines and one of the secrets of her everlasting stability: that great depth of keel, sixteen feet from the waterline where the workman stands. "We started out from Shelburne, Nova Scotia, in a gale of wind one night," recalled Captain Hynes, "and in a couple of hours she was vibrating so bad I thought it would knock the spars out of her. Thought we musta hit something. Went into Liverpool, got over the bar at the entrance all right, turned around and headed her for the railway, and gave it to her because there's not much more than a vessel length to spare and a terrific current in the harbor there. Made it, and hauled out, and found she'd lost a blade off the propeller."* JOHN CLAYTON PHOTO

trips he would make on *Adventure*. His brief log is the only such known in modern times and remains a documentary as unmatched as the photographs he took on that and subsequent trips.

Left Fish Pier at 2 p.m. on Monday, June 13, 1949, under power. Just off end of pier started hoisting mainsail. A few minutes later, foresail. They're used only for steadying ship. 3:45 p.m.: Off Boston Lightship. Making 8½ to 9 knots. Watches set for tonight are one hour six minutes each, two men on each watch, one quartermaster [helmsman] and one lookout. Considerable slop, and vessel rolling and pitching.

Tuesday, June 14: Up at 6:30 a.m. Late for breakfast which was steak, chops, potatoes, milk, coffee, tea, bread, rolls, muffins, salad, etc. Heavy fog which lifted a bit around 8:30. 11 a.m.: Dinner. 12:45 p.m.: Heavy rips around edge of Georges Bank. Takes 15 minutes to get through them. White caps all around. Fathometer showed 60 fathoms in rips. Will fish at high or low slack tide. Probably jog all night and make the first set about 4 or 5 a.m. 2:20 p.m.: Stopped engine. Now about ten miles on Browns Bank. On clear night should be able to see the light on Seal Island [off Cape Sable, Nova Scotia]. Jogging under sail alone. 4:30 p.m: Started baiting up. Cut bait into squares about two by two inches, three-quarters thick. Supper. 5:23 p.m.: All bait cut and started baiting trawls. 7:15 p.m.: All but four slow men finished baiting up. All watches 57 minutes all night. Very cold, started fire in cabin stove. 9 p.m.: Went to bed.

Wednesday, June 15, 12:30 a.m.: Up and taking watch until 1:45. Foggy as hell all night. Can't see the bow of the ship from the pilothouse. 5 a.m.: Breakfast. 5:18 a.m.: Dropped the first dory. 5:30 a.m.: All dories dropped. Loran position last night just on Browns, 5 p.m., was 42°48' north, 66°28' west. Loran position when dropped dories 5:20 a.m. today, 42°50' north, 66°04' west. 6:30 a.m.: Leo blew the vessel's horn to signal to start hauling. Two dories parted the groundline and had to be picked up to be towed back to buoys. 8:08 a.m.: Dory #6 in tow, lost groundline. Plenty of dogfish, about three out of seven hooks. 10:13 a.m.: Last two dories alongside to unload. 10:30 a.m.:Dinner. Headed westward under power. I counted too many dogfish here. 11:15 a.m.: Last dory dropped on second set. Only went westward several miles. 12:30 p.m.: Picked up two dories with busted groundline, towed back to buoys. Pea soup fog all morning. Can't see over a hundred feet. More dogfish this morning. Can hear them slap against the side of the dory whe they're being unhooked. This morning's set, about 12,000 pounds. 3:45 p.m.: Last dory picked up. Set this p.m. Hauled about 6,000 fish and many dogfish. 3:30 p.m.: Supper. 3:55 p.m.: Steering southwest by west, half west, to get away from the dogfish. 4:15 p.m.: Through cleaning fish, gutting, washing and icing. 6 p.m.: Loran, steering northwest edge of Georges Bank, 34 miles to go on southwest by west, half west. 8 p.m.: Heavy fog, cold as hell. Tonight's watch is one hour ten minutes each. Scheduled to start cutting and baiting up at 5 a.m., first set at 7 a.m. 10 p.m.: Change course to sou'west. Fog lightened a bit. 10:20 p.m.: Cut off engine at Loran position 42°10' north, 66°55' west. Jogging under sail the rest of the night. 10:30 p.m.: To bed. Trawlers all around in dense fog. Can't see a hundred feet.

Thursday, June 16, 4:30 a.m.: Up. 4:45 a.m.: Started cutting, baiting up. 5:30 a.m.: Breakfast. 6:10 a.m.: All trawls but one baited. Extra heavy fog again. 7 a.m.: First dory dropped. 7:18 a.m.: Last dory dropped. 8:10 a.m.: Blew horn to start hauling. Weather clearing in spots. 9:05 a.m.: In connection with placing telephone call, Leo told WOU Boston marine operator that we're 170 miles east southeast of Boston Lightship. Fog very thick. 10 a.m.: Picked up first dory with partial set. Dory full of fish. All of the dories followed first one with partial sets, full dories. 12:15 p.m.: Last dory alongside and fish forked over. About 30,000 pounds of fish from this set. 2:15 p.m.: All fish cleaned and stowed and the decks washed down. 3-5 p.m.: Slept. 6:05 p.m.: Started cutting and baiting up. Foggy continuously all day. 8:20 p.m.: First dory dropped. 8:30 p.m.: Last dory dropped. Had torches, smudge pots, in the bow. Only set one and a half tubs of trawl nights. No buoy. Used heavy weight and it's placed to hold the anchor down. [Evidently the dory served in place of the buoy.] Could not find buoy at night. They say a 10,000 pound set is very good here on Georges at night. 9:28 p.m.: Blew horn to start hauling. 10:58 p.m.: First dory alongside to unload fish. 11:33 p.m.: Last dory alongside to unload. About 10,000 pounds this set. 11:30 p.m.: Super supper, dinner or whatever you call it.

Friday, June 17, 12:15 a.m.: All fish dressed down. 12:30 a.m.: To bed. 5:30 a.m.: Under way. Men up. Had breakfast and baiting up. 6:30 a.m.: I got up. Foggy as hell again. 6:50 a.m.: Jogging around the spot where we were yesterday morning. 7:10 a.m.: Finished baiting up. 7:50 a.m.: Last dory dropped. Leo says we're right back on the spot where we were yesterday a.m. 8:50 a.m.: Blew horn. Start hauling. 9:25 a.m.: One dory alongside after parting groundline after hauling for lines. He in tow to buoy. For about 45 minutes had horn argument with beam trawler damn close to us. Did not see him at all. 11:20 a.m.: One dory alongside to unload partially. Has eleven lines left to haul. 1:15 p.m.: Last dory on board. This set about 20,000 pounds of fish. Been foggy all day, very. 1:30 p.m.: Dinner. 2:50 p.m.: Cleaned and iced down. 3:30 p.m.: Trawler which has been around us all day crossed our stern in light fog. She's a beam trawler, *Bonnie*, from Boston, dragging. 7:30 p.m.: Started baiting up. One and a half tubs per dory for tonight's set. Drifted about five miles east of this a.m.'s position this afternoon. 8:15 p.m.: Supper. 8:20 p.m.: Finished baiting up. 9:20 p.m.: Dropped first dory. 9:38 p.m.: Last dory dropped. 10:25 p.m.: Horn to start hauling. 11:45 p.m.: First dory alongside. Lost part of trawl. Has only a few fish.

Saturday, June 18, 12:45 a.m.: All dories but one in. Super supper. 1 a.m.: Going after missing dory. 1:05 a.m.: Last dory alongside. This set about 10,000 pounds. 1:35 a.m.: Fish dressed and iced. 1:40 a.m.: To bed. 6:40 a.m.: Started baiting up. 7:43 a.m.: Breakfast. 8:10 a.m.: Through baiting up. 8:50 a.m.: Last dory dropped. 10 a.m.: Horn to start hauling. We are in the position where we were last night, five miles west of yesterday's a.m., 175 from Boston Lightship. 10:10 a.m.: Dory blew horn for tow to buoy. Parted groundline. Two additional dories parted groundlines, had to be towed to buoys. 12:10 p.m.: First dory alongside to unload. 1:40 p.m.: Two dories missing. 2:05 p.m.: Last dory picked up. This set about 12,000 pounds. 2 p.m.: Dinner. 2:10 p.m.: Steering west half north, headed for South Channel. 2:50 p.m.: Fish dressed and iced. 6 p.m.:

Altered course to WNW. 8 p.m.: Leo told me we headed back to Boston on account of run out of ice. Had some left over in the hold which turned so soft it was no good. 8:30 p.m.: Ran out of fog for the first time in four days. Clear and calm seas. 11:30 p.m.: To bed.

Sunday, June 19, 6:30 a.m.: Up and a late breakfast. Beautiful day. 9 a.m.: Off Cape Cod and Highland Light. 11:15 a.m.: Off Plymouth. 2:30 p.m.: Docked at the Fish Pier after running through the Boston area yachting fraternity celebrating Maritime Day. Took cook and Frank Mayo in a taxi to Cambridge, cook to Central Square, Frank to Inman Square. Crew's share was $140. After withholding tax, net share was about $121.50 per man.*

John Clayton didn't think it worth mentioning in his log that *Adventure*'s facilities required merely climbing up to the top step of the gangway in bad weather and peeing on deck, or going over the rail in good, or using a bucket as required, for there was no such modern contrivance as a head on board. His skipper was vastly amused:

"So John gets the bucket and goes to the rail, holding on tight to the bucket, hauls it in half full of water, Well, the vessel was rolling quite a lot. We were steaming out against a sou'wester, going down to the South Channel. Anyway, old John puts the bucket down and takes his pants down and gets ready to go, and the vessel takes a little lurch, and the bucket slides right across the deck. He had to pull his pants up, chase the bucket over there and try it again. My God, the bucket skidded right down again. He finally came back and said, 'Leo, I can't do this. This is ridiculous, chasing that bucket all over the foredeck!' Finally he got the idea and he tied it down. But I laughed at him!"

Clayton the Chronicler, however, had the last laugh on old In-and-Out during a later trip in *Adventure*.

"One night we were jogging, and I went on deck about three in the morning. I never saw a brighter night in my life. From the horizon and 360 degrees around, nothing but stars right down to the water. Absolutely breathtaking. Leo crawled out of his bunk and came up to look around. Wanted to know what I was doing on deck.

"I said, 'Leo, take a look!' He got excited and said, 'Where? Where?' I said, 'Look all around!' And he said, 'I don't see nothing but a bunch o' goddam stars!'"

Time and tide were taking their toll.

Skippy, now fifteen, was too old and sick, as Clayton sadly noted in February 1951, to climb the gangway and could barely get around on deck. They carried her back ashore whence she came and took her to the animal hospital to be put to sleep.

For five weeks *Adventure* was laid up in Gloucester for engine overhaul. John

---

* According to John Clayton's log: "Vessel takes one-fourth gross stock, paying one-fourth cost of oil and trawl replacements. Crew share and share alike from balance after deduction of: 10% commission to skipper on gross plus 5% on supplies—food, trawl, etc."

John M. Clayton, the chronicler of the last of the dory trawlers.
The camera is the ancient Graflex with which he took the black and
white photographs of Adventure *and her men.* CLAYTON COLLECTION

Martins was laid up for three weeks after breaking a leg tendon in the dory. Another old one, rarely off the bottle now, turned up sober for a change, but there was no site for him.

Now that the press was looking over his shoulder with such morbid expectation, Leo Hynes extolled the superiority of dory trawling over dragging every chance he had, though he knew he was whistling in the twilight.

The beam trawlers kill more than they bring aboard, he would fulminate. The government should ban dragging during the springtime spawning, when the fish won't take the hook anyway, as a conservation measure that the wiser heads among the fishermen had long been urging. And look at the waste—not only of the

Stalwarts of a fading era, John Martins and Jake Flores. JOHN CLAYTON PHOTO

spawners but of the young and of the fish squashed in the packed cod, or business, end of the net. His last five trips alone, Captain Hynes told the *Fishing Gazette* in November 1951, had averaged 70,000 pounds, and the large and firm fish fetched a higher price than the dragger-caught ones. There was still plenty to be taken on a hook, besides, in spots inaccessible to the depredations of the beam trawlers.

The supreme irony of it, as far as her master could see, was that *Adventure* could go on practically indefinitely; it was not her age or the competition that was putting on the squeeze but the shortage of men, young men, able or willing to go in her. By the 1950s, most of his crew were over fifty—older than the Old Man. Lamented the *Fishing Gazette*: "It is too bad to see such a rugged body of men and their work passing; it seems like a mistake, in the face of their courage and enthusiasm."

Her skipper chomped on his cigar and explained to a Boston reporter that *Adventure* needed twenty-seven men to fish twelve dories, almost twice the crew of a beam trawler. And the trouble was that "now the kids are used to the nets. They can't work the dories. Can't bait the hooks or take in the lines and unhook the fish. It's not their fault. It's just that they haven't got the experience. That's another reason why line trawling is going out, but the main reason is the big crew."

Still they hung on. Henry Allen, Mark Almoral, and Edgar Babine quit to try beam trawling in January 1952. Allen reported back that he was making twice as much and working only six-hour shifts. Fred Thomas was seventy and ailing and going out on the same tide with his pal Skippy. He and Jake Flores had both been sick in the hospital and were back aboard, thin and weak. Two others showed up drunk, just in time for sailing. John Clayton was along that trip and found a "bunch of strangers I never saw before."

The old ways were breaking down before Leo's eyes. Spring of 1952 came around, and he told Clayton that Fred Thomas was back in the hospital, probably all washed up. He had to hire another engineer, thus ending the Thomas dynasty. Tom Bambury hurt his knee and had to stay home a trip. Leo Romaine and Pat Nolan were threatening to quit, fed up. The fishing was lousy. They were shorthanded, with only enough to man ten or eleven dories, including what Leo harshly called riffraff. Frank Mayo quit and bought a small dragger, to the hoots of the rest, who wanted to know what the hell did The Pimp know about dragging?

So after eighteen years of the old ways in *Adventure*, Hynes said the hell with it and laid plans in 1952 to build a modern steel longliner of sixty-five feet that would reel off the trawls from astern at eleven knots without anyone having to set foot in a dory. She would carry 65,000 pounds of fish and be the first such on the New England coast. The idea was that he and Lil would ultimately convert her to their retirement home afloat. So Leo Hynes and Phil Manta, who was seriously ill, put *Adventure* up for sale for $35,000, which seemed a reasonable figure, considering they had turned down $60,000 for her during the war.

Waiting for that last blast on the air horn, old timers Manuel Marshall, John Martins, Ellsworth Buchanan, and an unidentified veteran pass the time of a sunny day in the lee of the riding sail. JOHN CLAYTON PHOTO

Winter came and went, and Clayton, anxious about the Old Lady, was back the next March. It was now 1953. The litany of woes had intensified. The fishing was worse than ever, with low prices, high expenses, bad weather, and worse luck. John Meagher tripped and fell on deck, and they had to take him into Shelburne to the hospital. Flores and Romaine each cut off the end of a finger and were out of action for weeks. But Frank Mayo was back after one trip in his dream dragger; the old engine had given out, and he sold it.

They dropped their asking price for *Adventure* to $20,000 and turned down $18,000 from a party who wanted to convert her to coastal freighting. "When we have to sell her," Leo told John Bunker of the *Monitor* in a March 10 article that reads like an obituary, "I hope one thing doesn't happen. I hope they don't make a beam trawler out of her. She doesn't deserve a fate like that."

Adventure was on Georges on what her skipper thought might be her finale when the *Monitor* article appeared. He had postponed twice for lack of men and had sailed shorthanded at that: only nine dories. Someone calculated that the senior citizens he had along this trip averaged forty years at sea. And now she was the last, because the *Marjorie Parker*, which had been fishing out of Portland when they could put together a crew, had been chartered, for lack of one, to the government.

Adventure was the last of her class.

By the summer of 1953, Blount Marine in Warren, Rhode Island, had laid the keel of the Hynes longliner. She'd cost $67,000, for which Leo and Lil hocked just about everything, and would be launched in September.

With not a buyer on the horizon, Leo turned *Adventure* over to Mike O'Hearn while he fretted over every weld and bolt in his new craft, the first he would ever own outright. John Clayton came down to the Fish Pier in late July and logged: "*Adventure* looks a wreck. Needs paint all over." She sure did.

Clayton got the exit call from Old In-and-Out and was back in Boston on November 2.

> Leo planned two more trips before permanently laying up the vessel. Insurance had about expired. Company would not insure for less than an additional year. Leo said no soap. This a.m. took the vessel off Boston Lightship to dump a lot of junk, mattresses, etc. Back today, and tomorrow to Munroe's, up Chelsea, to tie up permanently.

Then the last entry in John Clayton's log of the auxiliary fishing schooner *Adventure*:

> November 3, 1953, Tuesday: Down early to the pier. Invited ourselves aboard for the last sail. Left the pier about 10:30 a.m. Leo Hynes, Leo Romaine. To Munroe's yard in Chelsea, where tied up along the pier, probably for good. Charges $200 a month to tie up, half for the use of the pier, the other for insurance.

In the nineteen years Leo Hynes and the boys fished *Adventure*, their worst was $96,000, their best $364,000. Their total exceeded $3,500,000. And Jeff Thomas's? Probably another half a million or more.

Conservatively, four million dollars worth of fish at the dealer's always-rock-bottom price in twenty-seven years—every last one baited up, hauled up, pitched up, dressed, iced down, and pitched out by hand.

End of era.

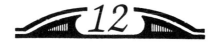

Bittersweet

This is the life I have known as far back as I can remember, when I was a kid growing up in the little fishing village called Bay l'Argent, Newfoundland. This is the life I love, and this is the life I shall continue to follow as long as I live or as long as I can find a crew to sail with me.

Leo Hynes, in the *Boston Post*

im Munroe's shipyard on the Chelsea shore was right where the Mystic River from the west unites with the Chelsea River, more an oversize tidal creek than a real stream, from the east. After flowing between the wharves of Charlestown and East Boston, the Mystic merges with the Charles River past the Boston waterfront and the runways of Logan Airport into Boston Harbor. The shipyard is a couple of blocks east of the soaring Tobin Bridge that links the city to the New England coast beyond. A hundred and fifty years and more ago the site was the terminus for the Winnisimmet Ferry, which served the same purpose in its day.

For the technologically retired dory trawler *Adventure*, however, Chelsea Creek was a bleak backwater where many a proud sea lady, having outlived what was presumed to be her usefulness, had been laid up against the better day that never came, to sink into the mud, forgotten and neglected, and expire. In other words, the end of the line, the boneyard.

For the Old Lady, a far cry from the cry of the gull and the Fish Pier and the heel of Browns. Faced with such a fate, better to have been broken up and fed into her own stove. The ultimate irony of it was that *Adventure* had not outlived her usefulness, only her men.

Never one to waste time looking over his shoulder, Leo Hynes beat a path between his home in the northern Boston suburb of Melrose and the Blount shipyard, down on the eastern shore of Narragansett Bay. *Sherry and Scott*, named for the first two grandchildren, took shape rapidly during the winter and was launched in a burst of bubbly before a crowd of two hundred well-wishers on June 19, 1954.

Instead of a crew of twenty-six, Captain Hynes took with him four former Adventurers: faithful Tom Bambury, now sixty-four, as cook, ex-draggerman Frank Mayo, John Martins, and Lawrence Doucette. For a time, Leo Romaine was along. The skipper's plan was to go after the usual fish, as he always had, and during the summer months the swordfish, but now with the longline.*

From the start they had trouble getting the hang of it and found that although the principle was the same, there was plenty of difference between setting two or three strings of trawl at a time from a fifty-six-ton vessel and one from a two-man dory. The most they could handle altogether was twenty-four tubs, and the trawl kept parting from the great extra strain, especially in a current. To add to his problems, Leo couldn't get the compass adjusted accurately when surrounded by so much steel.

Meanwhile, back in Chelsea Creek—battered, scraped, scuffed, rust-streaked, beat-up, weather-worn, and paintless—the Old Lady dozed at Munroe's, where her only keeper was a shore hand who climed aboard when she looked noticeably lower in the murk and pumped her out. As John Clayton bemoaned, she looked a wreck. But a still-pround one, because no amount of unavoidable neglect could conceal those classic lines or suppress the spirit of the handsome old schooner whose heart remained as stout as it was the day she was launched in 1926.

Nevertheless, there were few who ever had to do with her who would have give you a plugged nickel for her chances. So it is the more to be appreciated that she caught the eyes of a trio of men who had been partners since 1940 in what was then the very rough-and-ready business of carrying paying passengers on summer sailing cruises along the Maine coast in gussied-up old-time work schooners. Lying up there in the creek, dowdy and frowzled and growing unseemly grass on her bottom, *Adventure* aroused the interest of Donald P. Hurd, Dayton O. Newton, and Herbert Beizer, and they made an offer of $9,000, which was accepted because there were no others.

The "dude" schooner trade started up in Penobscot Bay in 1935 when the legendary Frank Swift—artist, craftsman, mariner, and mentor—took a covey of summer campers for a week's cruise on a coasting schooner of the sort that still

---

* Leo was ahead of his time. Highly successful longlining for swordfish was just in the offing then, and in retrospect he wished he had concentrated on that, which of course requires much heavier gear.

Old Maggie*'s sails ease* Adventure *through Maine waters at the start
of her windjamming career under Captain Dayton Newton.* SHARP COLLECTION

poked in and out of Maine ports in those days. They all had such a splendid time that the next season he chartered the little old coaster *Mabel* to carry more or less working passengers (hence "dudes") out of Camden for weekly cruises at twenty-five dollars a head, whence came the reference to "head" boats, or cattle boats less delicately, or skin boats least so.

Captain Swift ran a fleet of a dozen rehabilitated "windjammers"—his name for them—in the twenty-five years of his active involvement. Interrupted by the war, the pleasant commerce was still in its early growing stages when Don Hurd bought the Chesapeake Bay freighting schooner *Maggie*, eighty-seven feet long and seventy-five years old. He reconditioned her, and relocated her from Baltimore to Rockland, a few miles west of Camden, for her first exposure to sneakers in 1946. Hurd had been national director of the Red Cross for twenty-eight years and lived in Boothbay Harbor. "Newt" Newton taught music at Admiral Farragut Academy in New Jersey and took *Maggie*'s helm summers—until they spotted the *Adventure*.

By 1954 *Maggie* was eighty-three and worn out. Hurd and Newton got Leo Hynes to take *Adventure* from Munroe's back into the mother waters (oh, happy day!) and down to New Bedford, where the engine was removed to meet Coast Guard requirements governing fire hazards in the passenger schooner trade. They sold the engine, which helped to pay for the boat, got rid of the pilothouse, rebuilt the hatches, cleaned the pens out of the fishhold, scrubbed it, and filled it and the former engine room with staterooms between the main cabin bulkhead and the galley. They stripped most of the berths from the fo'c'sle to make room for more tables and seats. Except for minor repairs, the main cabin and galley were left much the same. From the cut-down masts they hung *Maggie*'s booms, gaffs, sails, and a good deal of her rigging, which gave *Adventure* the look of a seagoing bag lady.

Having cleaned her out, cleaned her up, and restored her to some manner of sail, her new owners presented *Adventure* with *Maggie*'s donkey engine for raising anchor, and her yawlboat to push her from here to there in the absence of air and Fred's diesel. All in great haste. And then they booked their first passengers on the illustrious Gloucester knockabout and sailed forth from Rockland for the summer of 1954.*

Adventure was still deep in her first hibernation on the Maine coast as her restless old ex-skipper steered her successor, the steel *Sherry and Scott*, across Emerald Bank. They were a hundred miles or so almost due east of Cape Sable, Nova Scotia, and had about thirty thousand pounds of fish on board. It was April 25, 1955. The new longliner was ten months old.

Late that day a southeast gale with forty-five-mile winds breezed in, and Leo though it best to head for Shelburne. He gave the helmsman a course of northwest by west, and, dog-tired, went below to lie down. He remembered that his last Loran bearing was on Roseway Bank.

They struck at three-thirty in the morning.

"When I heard the thump I was lying down with my oilskins on, hadn't intended to go to sleep but was sort of exhausted. I thought we'd hit the Lockeport buoy. I jumped up in the pilothouse and looked down in the engine room, and here was the water pouring in. It was a good thing she didn't stay on the ledge, which musta been a half mile offshore, because she went on in and hit the cliff.

"I turned the spotlight on. Lucky the batteries were up high, above the water.

---

* The history of the dude schooners is concisely set forth in *Windjammers of the Maine Coast*, written and illustrated by Harry W. Smith and published by Down East Books in 1983.

Didn't know where we were. I was trying to get a bearing when she hit the bottom and knocked me down, and I got up and started to put out the distress signals. There were about four frequencies, but the beam trawlers had their nets in and their radios off for the night. Found out later the Coast Guard picked it up in Boston. We had no radar.

"We were headed northeast toward the cliff with the wind southeast on our starboard beam. There were two dories on the lee side. Got one dory over and Tom Bambury in it, slacked it ashore by the painter and another rope on that. Hauled it back, and Frank Mayo got in and got ashore and was trying to bail it out when somebody hollered, 'Watch out! Big sea coming!'

"That's all I knew. I went overboard. I was standing in the coil of the rope attached to the painter. When I had gone to put on a life preserver, there was one in the bunk, but it was for a child, so I got one from the *Adventure* that I had put in the lazarette. It saved my life. The dory took off and hit the rocks and dumped Frank out. The rope was wound around my boot, and I went to the bottom and hit a rock. My God, I thought I was a goner! That line would have pulled my right leg off if I hadn't got it free! That's where I broke my ankle.

"I got in and got ahold of the kelp, but I couldn't hold on. I was exhausted. Frank and Tom were quite a distance apart. Tom finally went out in the undertow and grabbed me and got me in. I was laid out on the rocks for fifteen minutes before I could get my breath.

"There were still two more aboard, Martins and Doucette. They got a rope off the bow and floated it in, and Tom made it fast around a rock. I told 'em to tie a line around themselves and throw the end ashore in case they fell off the rope, and they shimmied ashore that way.

"We made our way up to the top of the hill. They dragged me, me dragging my foot, and there was an old farmhouse. The old lady had moved in just the day before with her granddaughter. She got me a blanket, and I stripped right off, trembling. We burned pieces of the old barn to keep warm. She didn't have any food. Feller looking to see if any lobster pots came ashore in the storm found the wreck, went up to the house and took us to the settlement in his truck. Nobody got back aboard of her, and she went to pieces in a week."

That's the way the dream ended, the fleeting life of the steel longliner *Sherry and Scott*, in the raging sea east of Lockeport against a cliff near Sable River, on a black and stormy night at least fifteen miles east of her destination. For all her compass problems, it appeared likely to Leo that the helmsman was steering northwest by north instead of northwest by west as he had directed, a full 22½ degrees off course.

"Leo has had many narrow escapes with the sea," Lil told the *Boston Globe* reporter when he called her at home in Melrose, "but this was the worst. Most of our life savings went into the *Sherry and Scott*. She was built to plans Leo had worked over and dreamed about for years. She was designed almost like a pleasure craft, and we were going to use her for just that when he retired next year."

Then she got in the car and drove to Nova Scotia to bring her husband home.

The wrecked dream was insured for $40,000, so they lost $27,000 of their life savings, as well as almost a year's worth of earnings while Leo was overseeing her construction.

His broken ankle was mending, but not his spirit, when Captain Hynes was invited by the new owners of *Adventure* to come down to Rockland that summer and take her cruising for them. That seemed to snap him out of it, and he so enjoyed the feel of the old wheel in his hands, the quiet power of sail that had pushed many a schooner along for him in his younger days, the pleasure of exploring a coast hitherto hurried past offshore, that he wished he had foreseen such a future for both of them himself. Yes, had Leo only known, he would have hung on to *Adventure* and taken her windjamming himself.

On the other hand, 180 degrees may have been too much of a course change to expect from old In-and-Out, the highliner to whom the challenge of it meant more than the money, the driven slavedriver, the master of men who lay awake in his bunk thinking about fishing and then dreamed of it when he dropped off to sleep.*

So after they tied up *Adventure* for another winter, and with all his plans knocked askew, Leo gritted his teeth and went beam trawling, that scorned crime against the ocean bottom for which a man who could think like a fish was much in demand. For close to ten years, until he reached the retirement age of sixty-five in 1965, he skippered various draggers out of Boston, including the *Patty Jean*, formerly *Lark II*, the successor to the Channel Express, his rival of days never to return.

The life was easier, the hours shorter, the pay better, the technology something to marvel at, but Leo didn't really take to it. "I brought in a lot of fish, but I tore up an awful lot of gear trying to fish my old spots." Ah, those familiar old spots, *Adventure*'s private Edens for the very reason that they were too rough for the draggers to risk their nets on.

Hynes retired, but not for long. Forever restless, he got a job in a restaurant, of all places, and then in a grocery store selling vegetables, of all things. It was a blessing, all right, to renew acquaintances with Lil and his two sons and his daughter and their spouses, and to play the old sea dog of a grandfather, but the sea call was always in his ears over there beyond the hills of Melrose and Peabody and the dales of Nashua, New Hampshire, where the Hyneses finally settled down.

* To mark the fiftieth anniversary of Captain Hynes's first great trip in *Adventure*, Jim and Pat Sharp arranged a party at the Blackburn Tavern in Gloucester on May 5, 1984. Among the celebrants were Leo and Lil, daughter Patricia, old shipmate Tom Fowler, Mike O'Hearn, and the author and his wife, Helen. Still robust at ninety-one, "Mike Dempsey" raised a glass with Leo Hynes, and they "made up" over their clash of the *Adventure*s forty-one years earlier. Veteran Boston waterfront reporter Bill Coughlin immortalized the occasion in the May 7 *Boston Globe* under the heading, "They gathered in Gloucester to swap tales of old sea voyages."

Leo was seventy-two, still keeping up with the century, when he passed the examination for his commercial license and went back to work for O'Hara Brothers, after forty years, as master of their small tanker, delivering oil to their vessels and the towboats and the harbor islands. For seven agreeable years, In-and-Out Hynes poked in and around Boston Harbor and his former haunts—busy, sociable, and content that he could still be at sea, in his own way, and at home too, a balance of both worlds at last.

In 1978 Leo Hynes quit the sea for good. Well, not quite. But more on that anon.

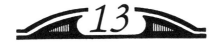

An Adventure Renewed

Ships that pass in the night, and speak each other
in passing,
Only a signal shown and a distant voice in the
darkness.

Longfellow

T he Old Lady in her hand-me-downs sailed without incident for ten years in the dude trade out of Rockland. It was a decade that saw a steady rise in the national popularity of Maine coast windjamming and a dramatic rise in the rate of rehabilitation of antique merchant sailing vessels that were sound, able and roomy enough to meet the Coast Guard regulations. And when it was no longer possible to track down recyclable old lumber coasters and brick carriers, the sounds of adze, saw, and mallet re-echoed across many a spruce-studded cove as the tide of renewed fascination with wooden boats and the building of them rose along the seaboard.

Not only was *Adventure* the only former fishing schooner among the windjammers (or any other working vessels anywhere, for that matter), but she was by far the biggest of the two-masters, the fastest in a breeze, and the deepest (drawing fourteen feet, two fewer than when she was fishing), which made her no mean challenge to navigate around the well-known and not-so-well-known pitfalls of the coastline. It happened that Captain Newt had a misadventure with one of these pitfalls that almost cost him his *Adventure* one day near the ferry landing at Islesboro, in Penobscot Bay, and swore off for life. The partners put her up for sale.

This time she did not languish long.

Maine folks are disinclined to admit it, but, just as in Gloucester, it's the influx of fresh corpuscles that keeps the old ones on the flow. Among these new bloods, arriving on the scene just as *Adventure* was in acute need of a transfusion, was a young Philadelphian, James W. Sharp.

As lead trombonist with Fred Waring's internationally famous Pennsylvanians, Sharp's father spent more time on the road than he cared to, and when he was home he liked nothing better than puttering around in his thirty-foot power cruiser—and, while he was at it, indoctrinating the boy, whose right leg had been permanently affected by a bout with polio in infancy, in the rehabilitative elements of seamanship. So the lad grew up messing about with boats.

Jim went to the University of Miami for a year and Oslo University in Norway for a summer. In 1954 his father died, and the son took over the finance business he had founded after retiring from the Waring group. For the next few years, between business courses at the University of Pennsylvania nights and running the family business days, he squeezed in time to sail a twenty-foot knockabout sloop on the New Jersey shore and race and cruise with friends in larger yachts.

All the while, the sea was working its insinuations on Jim Sharp. He was finding that less time was needed for the family business, somehow or other, and more for the boats. Around 1960 he and two friends bought the forty-five-foot *Malabar XI*, the only yawl of the thirteen *Malabars* that the great designer John G. Alden built for himself, and then sold, and one of the only three (two others were ketches) not schooner-rigged. They found her in Mamaroneck on Long Island Sound and sailed her to Georgetown, Maryland, far up the Chesapeake, where they chartered her off and on for three years to help with the expenses.

Along the way, young Sharp had a taste of what it was to be Captain Jim, and developed an appetite to learn more and make it official. He was about to cash in his share in *Malabar XI* on the prospect of sailing around the world with another friend in a three-masted schooner, when it fell through, and instead of his pals buying him out, he bought them out instead. Sailing *Malabar XI* to Florida, he chartered his first solid command around the Bahamas for a couple of years with the idea of getting into the cruise business with a larger vessel.

Captain Jim Nisbet, who took over Frank Swift's fleet when he retired, was looking for a mate he could groom to be skipper. He fell in with Sharp while in Miami and persuaded him to take on the Maine coast in the Swift schooners *Mattie* and *Mercantile* in the summer of 1963. For the young mariner, fresh from the blandishments of the Bahamas, the unexpected spells of fog and chill, the iceberg-

*Adventure's misadventure came in 1964 when she
wandered out of the Islesboro channel by the ferry landing.
Captain Newt was able to float her but decided to put
his schooner up for sale, and retire.* SHARP COLLECTION

cooled water, and the homeliness of the old gaffers, didn't add up to love at first sight. That winter he fled south again, but once back there, he couldn't get Maine out of his mind. The familiar bug had bitten.

The schooner *Stephen Taber* was up for sale, sixty-nine feet, able and handy and certainly well proven, for she was almost as old as those hills that hovered over Camden, having been built, like *Maggie*, in·1871, but as a brick carrier in New York. Later the *Taber* had coasted pulpwood around the Penobscot Bay region and was converted to a windjammer after World War II. The price was right, and it was Captain Sharp of the *Stephen Taber* for the Maine dude schooner season of 1964. It was also, the new skipper decided, the best move he'd ever made.

The best, however, was yet to come. But first, one more false start, this time in the form—and form is as far as it went—of a replica of the schooner *America* that sailed over to England and took the most famous of all cups away from the limeys in 1851. Jim wanted to build her and make her queen of the windjammers; he dug up her original plans and talked to a designer, but he could not get a Coast Guard decision on the required specs for the passenger trade, so he gave up the project.

The real queen, in the guise of a rather dowdy and underdressed Old Lady in black, was waiting in the wings.

Captain Jim had crossed tacks with her in the lee of Isle au Haut, reached in company with her through Merchants Row, and scudded with her down the Fox Islands Thorofare. He had gazed upon her dancing sheer with stricken eyes and yearned for her to be his own. Now she was *available*, and the price was right. He made the partners an offer. It was accepted, and early in 1965, at the age of thirty-one, James W. Sharp awoke one foggy and chilly Maine morning to find himself the fourth owner in thirty-nine years of the schooner *Adventure*.

"It was early March and pretty dismal. She was tied up down in Boothbay Harbor. The hatches were open and the snow was blowing down. Her bilges were frozen over, and there was an axe laying down there where they'd chopped through the ice to fix a pump to keep her afloat, she was in such poor condition. Snow drifts on deck, and the water leaking down through.

"They had aluminum doors on all the cabins. You'd slam one and it would rattle for ten minutes. When I was towing her from Boothbay to Rockland in May, I went down and unhinged every one of those aluminum doors from every cabin and brought it up and threw it overboard. Then I knew I'd *have* to make new wooden ones."

Jim was swamped that spring getting his Old Lady to Rockland to pick up the rest of her gear and then on to Camden to join the *Stephen Taber*. He took Orvil Young, Camden mariner and boat carpenter, aboard as his partner in Yankee Schooner Cruises. Young took over the *Taber*. Sharp sold *Malabar XI* in Florida and his business in Philadelphia, got married, and was so busy pooling his resources for the future of his overnight "fleet" that he could do no more than sail *Adventure* his first summer with her in the rig she came in.

At season's end, that fall of 1965, he sailed her to Rockland, hauled out her old spars, laid them on the wharf, and rolled up his sleeves.

For any but millionaires, the restoration of a wooden ship as large and as old as *Adventure* is a labor undertaken in installments. It can't be pulled off all at once. Resources of money and time, if not of the love of it, are limited, and you have to pay as you go, giving priority to the basics, then to the yearly catching-up as the income affords. And when that day arrives, and you think you're finally finished, and there she is in all her glory of yore for all the world to admire, then, like painting the Brooklyn Bridge, it's time to start all over on the steady maintenance that the mixture of old wood and new, salt water and fresh, wear and tear, deserves or demands, according to whether you earn and retain your mastery over your vessel or let yourself become her slave.

Adventure's great beam, the heavy athwartships crosspiece that makes the break in the deck, admitted an icepick to the handle in places. Sharp and his crew, with the essential advice of Orvil Young in all they tackled, spent days that winter of 1965-1966 stripping the deck back as much as twenty feet fore and aft of the rot in order to be able to stagger the plank butts. Then they pulled out the old beam, dragging its massive replacement across the harbor ice and jockeying it aboard—a tricky and slippery job. Then they put the deck back, like surgeons sewing up.

Considerable topsides planking had to be replaced. They hauled the new stock by the same route, balancing on skittery ice floes as they fitted and fastened. Ultimately thirty-five to forty percent of the outside planking above the waterline was replaced with white oak three inches thick. The old deck was showing the trampling, banging, scraping, and weathering of four decades and had the leaks to prove it; over a period, new white pine, likewise three inches thick, was laid from aft of the main cabin to the foremast. The waterways edging the deck at the base of the bulwarks were renewed; so were most of the stanchions and the rails. All the deck structures but the cabin trunk, the original Stoddart wheel and gear, and the original Reed windlass—another Gloucester-made fixture of antiquity—were replaced. A second forward companionway was built down through the forward fish hatch.

Sharp's most dramatic move restored to *Adventure* the lofty profile she first wore to sea, a fair approximation of the reach of spar and spread of sail that she must have carried in those early years when Jeff Thomas relied mainly on the wind.

Having extracted Leo's old topped mainmast and the foremast Newt put in ten years back, and laid them on the wharf alongside *Maggie*'s sundry sticks, the enthusiastic new owner embarked on the old nautical spar game, Who's Standing on the Gaff?

First, he ordered a new mainmast of Oregon fir, ninety-two feet long, eighty-two above deck, and nineteen inches thick at shoulder height. Roughing out with broadaxe and adze and finishing with the electric plane, Sharp reshaped the old seventy-seven-foot mainmast into the new foremast of the same length, eighteen inches through. Newt's foremast was already rotting where the ironwork went through the masthead; Jim slimmed it down from eighteen inches to twelve, tapered the ends, and turned it into a sixty-foot main boom, thereby avoiding the rot (it has since been replaced by a new sixty-five-footer). Next he made a forty-two-foot main gaff out of *Maggie*'s old main boom. Three or four years later he turned her old main gaff into a forty-two-foot maintopmast, which raised the head of her new topsail 110 feet above the water. With topmast sent down enough to clear, *Adventure* could sail under the Deer Isle bridge by a hair and thus through Eggemoggin Reach.

Below, berths were installed for captain and wife, mate and two hands, cook and a brace of helpers, and thirty-seven passengers among cabin, staterooms, and forepeak. There was just room to tuck an undersized but otherwise upright piano in the space left over from where Fred Thomas had tossed the wrenches around, and up aft of the galley a trio of heads in place of a trio of buckets. The miniature upright with shortened keyboard was placed athwartships of the space previously occupied by a parlor organ and converted to "Cabin Small." The piano was tracked

The thrill of his life came to Gordon Thomas, the historian of the schooners, the day in 1971 he took Adventure's *old A.P. Stoddart wheel in hand and sailed her down Penobscot Bay on a sentimental journey with Captain Sharp. Eleven knots she knocked them off, the vessel Jeff's son had named almost half a century earlier. SHARP COLLECTION*

down by *Adventure*'s most faithful passenger, Helen Hawkins of Huntington, New York (forty or forty-one trips as of 1984—she had lost count—and seven in *Roseway*).*

The continuous passageway amidships is a distinct amenity not to be permitted in another wooden passenger vessel. Nor will another wooden ship of *Adventure*'s burden again see service in the American trade. The Coast Guard has decreed a 100-ton limit on new wooden windjammers, 100 feet tops, and requires fixed watertight compartments in modern vessels—so no more dry passages from bunk to chow when it's raining up on deck.

To make up for her years in fisherman's black, Sharp gave the Old Lady a dress coat of white reminiscent of the *Elizabeth Howard*, Grey Ghost of the olden days. *Maggie*'s old yawlboat was spent, so he had Elmer Collemer of Camden build a stubby diesel launch, *Hercules*, for nudging its mistress around in the calms and tight spots. Malcolm Brewer crafted a pair of dories that Jim nested on the port side and tagged with impish brevity, *PB* and *J*, after the components of a popular sandwich. These gave way, after several years of service, to a seine boat, the kind the fishermen once rowed like madmen, feeding out their net around what they hoped was a skittish school of mackerel. Passengers on *Adventure* who just couldn't seem to get their signals straight in some otherwise placid Maine backwater dubbed it the *Spastic Spider*.

In 1970 Captain Sharp happened upon one of those classic Whitehall pulling boats with wineglass stern and graceful lines, built in Boston and surely at least seventy years old, abandoned behind a privy in North Haven, alders poking up between the planking. He restored it, named it *Nannie*, and hoisted it aboard.

Such nautical nicknaming, once begun, opened Pandora's hatches. Anthropomorphism ran rampant among passengers and crew. Up forward, the galley may be the nominal domain of the cook and command post of Pat Sharp, who oversees everything on board that the skipper doesn't, but the absolute dictator is Mame, the massive, black, squat, backside-beware Shipmate woodstove of the old fishing days, hot heart of the whole operation. Jeremiah is the bellows devised by an ingenious ally of the cook to fan Mame's flame, and Heathcliff, the red-hot water tank whose pipes insinuate themselves among Mame's hidden innards.

On deck, Bertha is a gasping, braying donkey engine that can be cranked by the knowing hand into explosive action to run the aged windlass and slowly, interminably, raise the dripping anchor. Beulah, a smaller version of the cursed and cajoled make-and-break engine of sixty years ago, is a compact pump, paroled by the skipper from an indeterminate sentence in a cemetery emptying rainwater from freshly dug graves. It was brought on board in 1984 to replace the more primitive

---

* Helen threw a blanket over her find and transported it to Camden in 1980. On a side road she ran into a Maine state police roadblock on the lookout for an escapee from the state prison at Thomaston. Skeptical of her piano story, the trooper drew his gun, approached cautiously, and whipped off the blanket. A retired art teacher, Mrs. Hawkins has left her mark on *Adventure* with dozens of relief carvings and signs, including the schooner's familiar logo.

but younger handshaking types beside the mainmast. Beulah is a 1½-h.p. Edson #3 built by the Domestic Engine and Pump Co. of Shippensburg, Pennsylvania, circa 1912. An *Adventure* loyalist, Charlie Finn of Holliston, Massachusetts, found it in Holyhood Cemetery in Brookline, outside of Boston, in 1983. He and his twin brother, Richard, trucked it to Camden in barter for his 1984 berth—for himself and his bass fiddle, Bertha (not related to the donkey engine), which he had lugged along on several trips in literal response to the cruise brochure's invitation to "bring your musical instrument."*

Almost overnight, wherever she sailed with a spanking breeze on her beam, or whatever secluded cove or busy harbor she entered majestically for the evening, the white Old Lady of the ghostly fishing fleets commanded the scene. Wherever they talked about the good old times when wood was wood and sail was sail and men were iron—not all so good, as we have seen—the word spread that the last of the Gloucester schooners was really and truly back on the wind.

Now it came to pass in the rarefied stratosphere of the yachting world that Rudolph Shaeffer, brewery magnate and yachtsman, was infected in 1966 by the same bug that had bitten Jim Sharp (who enjoyed a low immunity to the boating delirium) two years earlier. This was, in layman's language, simply the American strain of the bug that had driven Sidney Oland, the Canadian brewer, in a fever of promotional nostalgia the year before *that*, to build a replica of the Lunenburg champion *Bluenose*. Captain Shaeffer's result was more palpable than Captain Sharp's: not *Columbia* or the *Gertrude L. Thebaud*, for the Canadians flatly refused to race *Bluenose II*, but a handsome reissue of the schooner *America* after all. She was launched in May 1967 at Boothbay Harbor.

An attractive but not very exciting exercise in conspicuous consumption, someone must have suggested: Why not a rerun of that Olympian contest when the original crossed to England and beat Britain's best across the line?

And so a race was got up—"fixed," in a manner of speaking—on the sixth of June, 1967, off Maine, between Rudy Shaeffer's shining new *America* and Jim Sharp's grand old *Adventure*, chartered and renamed *Brilliant* for the occasion, which was a television special entitled "Sail to Glory."

The overriding challenge of the day, as it turned out, was to hold the bigger *Brilliant/Adventure* back, for she was the longer of the contestants by sixteen feet on the waterline. It was not easy. Jim was quoted in the *New York Times* account: "The *America* kept her engine running all during the race, which helped, but not enough. Suddenly I got a frantic order on the walkie-talkie to 'slow down that schooner!' I

---

* The ambience of an *Adventure* cruise, above decks and below, where Dee Carstarphen ruled the galley for several seasons—and a bookful of irresistible windjammer recipes that resulted therefrom—are presented by her in delightful and illustrated detail in *Windjammer World: A Down East Galley-Eye View*, published by Down East Books in 1979.

managed to stop laughing long enough to answer, 'Don't know how—this thing hasn't got any brakes!' Somehow everything worked out."

And somehow, one more ship that had passed others by in the night kept crossing Jim Sharp's horizon. This time it was the old, ice-beaten, eighty-eight-foot schooner *Bowdoin*, built in 1921 for Admiral Donald B. MacMillan to take him on his numerous arctic expeditions.

Bowdoin had been laid up at Mystic Seaport in Connecticut and was deteriorating for lack of funds to restore her. In 1968 Sharp offered to shape her up and put her to work as a windjammer. It was agreed. He towed her to Camden for extensive repairs and sailed her down to Provincetown just in time for the old explorer to feast his eyes before he died at ninety-four. Back in Maine Jim added *Bowdoin* to his and Orvil's fleet under charter until 1974, when age again overtook her, and the Bowdoin Schooner Association launched a full-scale restoration at Bath, with the object of educational and scientific voyaging.

Barely had Jim bid goodbye to *Bowdoin* when what from all the wide Atlantic should the tide bring practically to his bathtub but the old schooner *Roseway*, the same launched by the James yard a few months before they laid *Adventure*'s keel—the same vessel whose leftover timbers were worked into *Adventure*'s very frame. *Roseway* was a yacht until 1941, then on constant cruise in Boston Harbor, meeting ships for the pilots until they decided they needed a smaller and more modern craft and put her up for sale in 1975.

The Pilots Association had spared nothing on *Roseway*'s maintenance. Sharp and Young couldn't resist her. She was in the classic Gloucester schooner mould, a powerful hull of striking sheer with her straight stem and long bowsprit. Although ten feet shorter than *Adventure*, she could manage an equal payload of thirty-seven passengers. To swing the deal, they regretfully sold the much smaller *Stephen Taber*, then 104 years old and going strong.*

Captain Young took over the old pilot schooner, and they dressed her in a distinctive suit of tan sails. Because she had two engines, they were able to star *Roseway* in three Tall Ships parades. The first was the Bicentennial at New York in 1976, then the Boston encore in 1980. In 1981 Alan Talbot, a Camden lad who had come up through the hawsepipe from cabin boy in the *Taber* at fifteen, took command of her. In 1984 captains Talbot and Sharp sailed *Roseway* to Halifax in company with the chartered sixty-three-foot Alden schooner *When and If*, the postwar dream that was never realized for the man who had her built, General George S. Patton, Jr.

---

* Captain Sharp doesn't have much immunity to the towboat fever, either. He has owned several, the latest a compact old churner from Baltimore that he acquired at a forced sale and restored to usefulness. He holds a 300-ton license and squires his fleet around when needed from the pilothouse of *Port Assist*, with occasional off-season stints skippering the big tugs on the big jobs for the big city.

■

Back to *Adventure*, for a friendly if frisky Fate had no intention of letting her not live up to her name. The inspiration for her, as we have seen, came to Captain Jeff from his satisfaction with the looks and performance of that able McManus knockabout, the *Oretha F. Spinney*, which he fished for Captain Lem Spinney from 1923 to 1925. After Lem took her back, Jeff had the James yard borrow her lines for *Adventure*.

Ten years passed, and in 1937 Metro-Goldwyn-Mayer set about filming *Captains Courageous*, Rudyard Kipling's memorable novel of Gloucester fishing under sail, with Spencer Tracy, Freddie Bartholomew, Lionel Barrymore, and Melvyn Douglass, for which they required a genuine Gloucesterman to take the part of the heroic fictional schooner *We're Here*. The *Spinney* was more than available, this being the Depression, and she could make more money acting than fishing.

After passing her screen test with colors literally flying, she sailed around to the West Coast, where many of the scenes were being shot. All the while, Leo Hynes and the boys were doing the real fishing in her sister back east.

When the shooting was over, Cinderella was mothballed by MGM at Long Beach and forgotten. Four more years passed, and in 1941 she was found by the blond young giant Sterling Hayden, who also had figured there was more money in acting than fishing and was fresh from starring in his first motion picture.

Hayden was more master mariner than matinee idol by nature, having gone dory trawling on the *Gertrude L. Thebaud* and then having served as mastheadman in her against *Bluenose* in 1938 before his discovery by Hollywood. He bought the *Spinney*, organized a voyage freighting in the Caribbean, endured crew troubles, cargo damage, head winds, and rough seas that worked her old seams alarmingly, sold her down in the islands, and returned to the States in some disgust.

To tell a long story twice, precisely forty years after the *Oretha F. Spinney* played the *We're Here*, her sister *Adventure* was drafted for the same part in the second filming of *Captains Courageous*, this time off the Maine coast. Designed for theatrical release abroad, this film was also shown on television in the United States.

It was spring of 1977. Antoinette Productions (Norman Rosemont, producer) chartered *Adventure* and retained her skipper as expert consultant. First the art crew arrived in Camden and put in three weeks "aging" her, repainting topsides black, daubing fake rust and gurry stains in the right places, and installing a prop of her original fo'c'sle with such care for Jim's paneling and paintwork that not a nail was driven; they used wedges.

Then three weeks of shooting by the production crew, which had quite different notions of verisimilitude. Early every morning Captain Jim and his gang got *Adventure* underway for location out in the bay, where they would be joined by the camera boat, a fifty-foot power cruiser, and the actors, already drowsy from Dramamine and not feeling too dramatic in contrast with the stability of the studio.

*Hauled for her spring outfitting at Samples
boatyard, Boothbay Harbor.* NEAL PARENT PHOTO

Lively as ever, Adventure *bowls along Penobscot Bay on a windjammer day.* NEAL PARENT PHOTO

But after a while they found their sea legs and were rejecting the fast taxi and sailing back to shore at the end of the day's work with *Adventure/We're Here* and joining in the galley songfests.

Jim was half sardonic, half amused, by the experience:

"One day it was blowing hard, not much good for shooting anything else, and I told the director that now was the time to get the race scene between *Adventure* and *Roseway*. I'd been suggesting that they get it from a helicopter instead of from a boat bouncing all around, for a long time, and I tried to press it again. Finally, after half the day was over, they decided they would, but they had to put the camera on the camera boat.

"Well, it was jumping and bounding and throwing spray all over, and of course the schooners were banging along through the waves and throwing spray, and it was blowing like the dickens. And one of the cameras fell off the top of the camera boat and broke, but they had another hundred-thousand-dollar one along and could use that.

"They got a hell of a lot of footage that day, but when they came to look at it they couldn't use ninety-nine percent of it because it was jumping all over the place."

After the shooting was all over, the perpetrators vanished, and Jim and his crew had a scant three weeks to disassemble the prop fo'c'sle, paint over the fake rust and gurry stains, redo her topsides in gleaming white, and, turning the tables on history once again, change *Adventure* back for the second time in her career from a dirty dory trawler to a winged windjammer as the curtain rose on another season of wafting along the coast of Maine.

In his later years Captain Hynes has customarily sailed on the last September cruise of the season in his old cabin in his old schooner as Captain Sharp's honored guest. In 1981 the author was along too, and one exchange, as we were gamming down there, fogbound in Northeast Harbor, went like this:

The Queen of the Windjammers, minus dories, tubs of trawls, gurry kids, Red Jacks, and whiskered faces, ambles by a Maine island in August 1982. The Spastic Spider is snugged down where a nest of dories once occupied the deck. The fo'c'sle companionway behind the foremast is unchanged. A fresh water barrel sits beside it. The flat galley scuttle has a new skylight, and just aft of it, the forward fish hatch is now a second gangway. ANDREW R. COEYMAN PHOTO

Leo: Fishing? A rugged life. Not fit for a human being.

Joe: Any compensations?

Leo: None, I guess. You'd think about the old dances in Nova Scotia.

Joe: If you had it all to do over?

Leo: I'd stay in the merchant marine. I was a quartermaster when I left and probably would have got up to bos'n.

Jim: I'll bet you'd have stayed a fisherman.

Leo: Well, it was a challenging thing.

Joe: Yeah, if you were a skipper, and how many made skipper?

Leo: Not many.

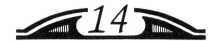

The Captivating Coasts

The breeze being fair and steady, we held on our course without stopping, till, at 6 p.m., we reached Owl's Head, an exceedingly picturesque promontory where a large white lighthouse crowned a high rock rising abruptly from the water. Here we anchored in a broad channel between the mainland and two islands, amid a fleet of vessels. This channel is much frequented by coasters and fishermen, and five hundred sails have been seen passing Owl's Head in one day.

Robert Carter, *A Summer's Cruise on the Coast of New England*, 1864.

aine's has always been a working coast, and, like the hard-bitten shores of Nova Scotia and Newfoundland way farther down east, its outports are a sight handier by water than by land. With a big enough block and tackle at either end, and the will power, you could straighten out that jagged coastline and stretch it to Florida if you wanted to—it's that indented with bays and salt rivers following the glaciated gorges that cut roughly north and south.

The deepest of these old gashes in the wilderness is Somes Sound, which knifes up through the middle of Mount Desert Island between Southwest and Northeast harbors. The only true fjord in America, they say. So straight-down deep that you can drop your anchor in fifty feet of ice water in Valley Cove almost close enough to jump ashore on a blueberry bush for a climb up the steep face of Saint Sauveur

Mountain and look back down on God's blue water and green islands just where He put them.

In sailing times it was miles and a day or two handier than by land to poke into some landing around the tip of one of those fir-girt fingers of granite, and take on a deckload of fresh-sawed board from the forest that still spills into the sea on every hand, and sail off with it for wherever—Portland, Boston, Providence, New York, or even Gloucester, which is where ninety-five years ago a couple of schooner-fuls were dropped off on an Eastern Point beach to build the author's home.

The coasting skippers of the hard old days—calloused, gallused, unbathed, and unshaved—dickered, swapped, and no doubt on occasion swiped anything and everything they could lay their horny hands on for whatever profiteth, from shingles to salt fish, paving blocks to pianos, hooked rugs, red rum, potatoes, chickens, derby hats, bricks, harmonicas, and Bibles.

The way of life was of lore, and in the latter days some of the less smelly, squawky, and skinflinty aspects of the lore have been adopted as a way of life.

In that sense of direct inheritance, the few venerable coasters among today's windjammers, from wherever they were launched, are the legitimate heirs to Maine's carefully nurtured but still credible tradition of pokin' 'long, pickin' up th' buoys in th' dam thick, mebbe nosin' up Tenants way with th' toyde, when an' if it scayles up, fer thet lot o' ax han'les Fred promised an' a decklud o' hay, *eff* th' gol ram sun'll jes' peek aout long 'nuff t' droy th' fethahs on a shag.

Those sharp, uncanny, old-time coasting skippers could, if they had to, sail their squat schooners (and some not so squat, such as the five- and six-masters of the great white Palmer fleet carrying coal by the thousands of dirty black tons along the seaboard) in the sweat off a pitcher of iced tea on a hot night in the dark without ever touching bottom. They knew every ledge and inlet and sounding worth paying attention to on the tangled coast like a dirt farmer knows his digs.

Next to the coastin' among Maine's maritime pursuits were the fishin' an' th' lobsterin'. The lobstering outgrew the fishing because in those days 'most any fool could catch lobsters in every rocky nook and cranny of the most convoluted coast this side of the Atlantic in 'most anything from his hands to a Jonesport thirty-six-footer. While the fish—well, there were no sizable ports with proper rail connections beyond Portland, whose slightly closer proximity to the Nova Scotia banks was more than offset by Gloucester's and Boston's to Georges and the South Channel. Not to mention the remoteness of the Maine coast from the major markets by sea and land and the sparseness of its population, for both of which attributes the sparsest population thanks its lucky stars every dawn from September to June.

Opposite: **Adventure *reaches out the Western Way from Mount Desert Island and the hills of Acadia National Park.*** JEFF DOBBS PHOTO

The Captivating Coasts 169

Still, Maine has a respectable commercial fishing tradition out of Portland, which waved goodbye to its share of dory trawlers out past the Lightship over the years, and Boothbay Harbor, haven and baiting station for the vast fleet of jiggers and seiners that once harassed the mackerel in the summer, and the remote cul-de-sacs of the sardine such as Port Clyde, where the canneries still pack 'em in.

Along with the coasting and the fishing and the lobstering, all of which spelled work but provided their satisfactions for the natives, and still do, was cruisin'—yes, just cruisin'—more along the leisurely line to be sure, sort of the Boston influence, but if Calvinistically enough adhered to, productive of its own surprisingly similar satisfactions, then and now.

Cruising, in all its subtle distinctions from yachting, is that upon which one sets out with compatible companions in a well-found and well-stocked cabin sailboat of proven sea ability for a poke-along coasting voyage of several days or preferably weeks, dropping the hook where the mood beckons, the spot beguiles, or the weather dictates, with no larger object than to get somewhere, anywhere, or nowhere and back in one piece with a minimum of fuss and a maximum of seamanship, ingenuity, cookery, and conviviality before the vacation comes to a regrettable end.

The effect of encountering the Maine coast for the first time in a cruising boat was celebrated for the first time a century and a quarter ago by a convivial newspaperman named Robert Carter in his discursive gem, *A Summer Cruise on the Coast of New England*. Always "Carter's Coast" to its devotees, this alongshore Baedeker describes in the freshest of detail the jolly and frequently hair-raising cruise that the Author and his singular shipmates—the Skipper, the Pilot, the Artist, the Assyrian, and the Professor—accomplished in the sloop *Helen* from Provincetown to Bar Harbor in the year 1858 at a charter of $7.50 a day. They have just discovered the sparkle of Casco Bay, where the ruggedness of Maine begins:

> It is doubtless safe to say that there are at least three hundred isles and islets, beside many bold and picturesque headlands and peninsulas, so that scarcely anywhere else in the world can you find a more varied or more lovely commingling of land and water.
>
> The shores of the islands and the promontories are mostly covered with woods of maple, oak, beech, pine and fir, growing nearly to the water's edge, and throwing their shadows over many a deep inlet and winding channel. It is impossible to conceive of any combination of scenery more charming, more romantic, more captivating to the eye, or more suggestive to the imagination. No element of beauty is wanting. Many of the islands are wildly picturesque in form, and from their woodland summits you behold on the one hand the surges of the Atlantic, breaking almost at your feet, and on the other the placid waters of the bay, spangled by gems of emerald, while in the distance you discern the peaks of the White Mountains.

A hundred and twenty-six years passed, and there was a September day in 1984, the first crisp day of the last cruise of the season, when the wind freshened from the southeast. *Adventure* poked her bow out of Camden under the excited urging of the yawlboat. The Skipper had along, among others, the Old Pilot, an Artist, a Professor, and the Author. Beyond the headland, the southeaster steadied and fluffed up a few whitecaps on the bay.

Haul away on the falls, and up to the davits with the yawlboat.

"Come on, you slackers!" roared the Skipper, and the rest of his passengers and his stalwart crew jumped to the halyards, not excluding the gentle Professor, and up rose the flapping mainsail. Then the foresail and the jumbo and the jib, and as she leaned into it now and began to limber up the old joints—and how they creaked!—aloft with the lad to the crosstrees to unstop the topsail.

Suddenly her kite was flying, and you could feel the extra surge through the soles of your feet and your eardrums, deck and wake.

It piped up, and it piped up, and she lay into it on her starboard reach, sheets twanging, lee shrouds limp and dangling, easing herself into the slow swells and up over them. Sizzling cascades of spray split away from her knifing, nosing, knockabout bow, and the froth and the bubbles and the foam and the green gurgling of the sea hissed along her quarter, boiling, roiling, rushing away astern.

It piped up, and it piped up. The Artist and the Author watched in wonderment. The Skipper eyed his quarter wake, and glanced aloft, and gave his wheel a touch and his cap a tug. "Fourteen knots. She's doing fourteen! Fast as she can go."

The Old Pilot was perched on the weather side of his old cabin trunk in his big sweater and *his* cap, and felt her tear through the water underneath him and grunted to himself. Fourteen knots. With a hunnert thousand o' fish down in the hold, she'd have been rail under doin' fourteen, the Atlantic Ocean pourin' right up over the deck to the port-side dories, and the gang chasin' down the sheets and buoy kegs gone adrift.

Bar Harbor up ahead.

A thing alive? You bet your Red Jacks she was, and all hands sensed it, and shared what she shared with the wind and the wave.

Having worked so hard so long, and seen such hardship and love and beauty and joy and sacrifice and gain and loss, and survived it all, the knockabout schooner *Adventure* had no doubt earned the pleasure of providing very little else but pleasure along the captivating coasts of her adventurous old age.

Bibliography

"*Adventure* Goes on a Dory Trawling Trip!" *Fishing Gazette*, November 1951.

"*Adventure* and *Marjorie Parker* the Last Two Dorymen Left." *Maine Coast Fisherman*, February 1952.

Babson, John J. *History of the Town of Gloucester*. 1860. Reprinted with introduction and historical update by Joseph E. Garland. Gloucester, Mass.: Peter Smith Publisher, 1972.

Bunker, John. "Sailors Shun Dory Fishing." *Christian Science Monitor*, March 10, 1953.

————."Trawler Back in Hub from Fishing Banks." *Christian Science Monitor*, June 9, 1949.

Carstarphen, Dee. *Windjammer World: A Down East Galley-Eye View*. Camden, Me.: Down East Books, 1979.

Carter, Robert. *A Summer Cruise on the Coast of New England*. 1864. Reprinted as *Carter's Coast of New England*. Somersworth, N.H.: New Hampshire Publishing Co., 1969.

Chapelle, Howard I. *The American Fishing Schooners 1825–1935*. New York: W.W. Norton, 1973.

Clayton, John M. *Log of fishing trips aboard* Adventure, *1949-1953*. Manuscript. (Mrs. John M. Clayton).

Connolly, James B. Letter to Gordon W. Thomas, May 27, 1952. (Jeffrey Thomas II).

Coughlin, William P. "Last of the Dory Fishermen." *Boston Globe*, November 8, 1981.

Fifield, Charles Woodbury, Jr. *Along the Gloucester Waterfront*. Gloucester, Mass.: 1955.

Garland, Joseph E. *Lone Voyager*. 1963. Reprinted, Rockport, Mass.: N.B. Robinson, 1984.

———.*Down to the Sea: The Fishing Schooners of Gloucester*. Boston: David R. Godine, 1983.

Gloucester Mutual Fishing Company records. (Cape Ann Historical Association).

Hayden, Sterling. *Wanderer*. New York: Alfred A. Knopf, 1963.

Hynes, Lillian. Family scrapbook.

Mesquita, Joseph P. *Statement of Capt. Joseph P. Mesquita of the sch.* Francis J. O'Hara, Jr., *regarding the loss of that vessel August 20, 1918*. (Joseph P. Mesquita, Jr.)

Olson, John S. Letter to Joseph E. Garland, August 18, 1984.

Parker, John P. *Sails of the Maritimes*. North Sydney, N.S.: 1960.

Pierce, Wesley G. *Goin' Fishin'*. Salem, Mass.: Salem Research Society, 1934.

Procter, George H. *The Fishermen's Memorial and Record Book*. Gloucester, Mass.: Procter Brothers, 1873.

Ship Registers of the District of Gloucester, Mass., 1789–1875. Salem, Mass.: The Essex Institute, 1944.

Sisson, William. "Highliner King Recalls Old Catches." *Soundings*, May 1984.

Smith, Harry W. *Windjammers of the Maine Coast*. Camden, Me.: Down East Books, 1983.

Story, Dana A. *A Catalog of the Vessels, Boats and Other Craft Built in the Town of Essex 1870 through 1980*. Based on the research of Lewis H. Story. Essex, Mass., 1984.

———.*Frame-Up!* Barre, Mass.: Barre Press, 1970.

Story, Dana A., and John M. Clayton. *The Building of a Wooden Ship*. Barre, Mass.: Barre Press, 1971.

Thomas, Gordon W. *Fast and Able*. Gloucester, Mass.: Gloucester 350th Anniversary Celebration, Inc., 1973.

Thomas, Jeffrey F. Letters to Florence Thomas Wylie, January 6 and 12, 1934. (Jeffrey Thomas II).

Tod, Giles M.S. *The Last Sail Down East*. Barre, Mass.: Barre Publishers, 1965.

White, Stephen A. "The Arichat Frenchmen in Gloucester: Problems of Identification and Identity. *New England Historical and Genealogical Register*, April 1977.

Willoughby, Malcolm F. *Rum War at Sea*. Washington, D.C.: U.S. Government Printing Office, 1964.

Yankee Schooner Cruises News. Box 696, Camden, Me. 04843. Yankee Schooner Cruises.

Miscellaneous Sources

Boston Globe
Boston Herald
Boston Post
Gloucester Master Mariners Association yearbooks
New York Times
North Shore Magazine of Essex County Newspapers

Index

*Numbers in boldface refer to black-
and-white photographs.*

Portland to Bar Harbor Maine

Adventure's Cruising Areas

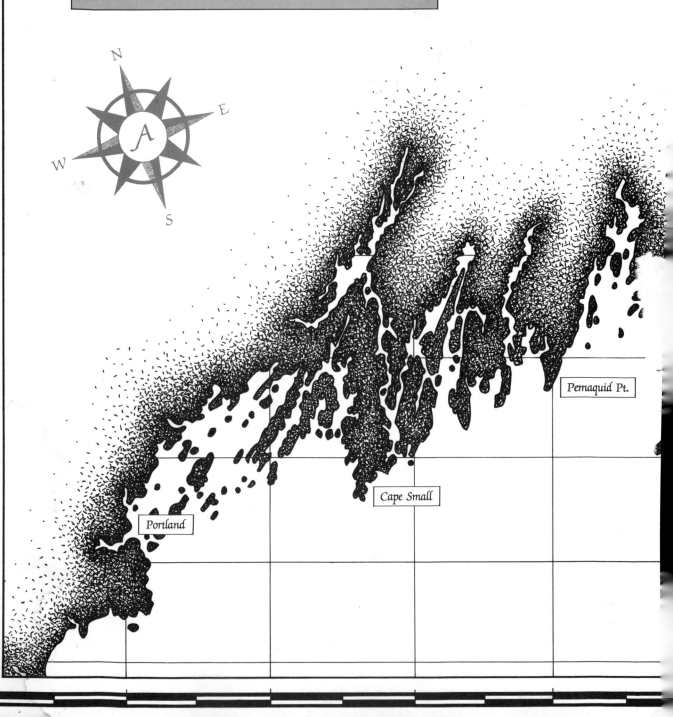

Pemaquid Pt.

Cape Small

Portland

387 Gar
Garland, Joseph E.
Adventure: queen of the wind-
  mmers